NINE PRINCIPLES

of

LITIGATION AND LIFE

NINE PRINCIPLES *of* LITIGATION AND LIFE

MICHAEL E. TIGAR

AMERICAN BAR ASSOCIATION
**Defending Liberty
Pursuing Justice**

SECTION *of* LITIGATION
AMERICAN BAR ASSOCIATION

Cover design by ABA Publishing.

The materials contained herein represent the opinions and views of the authors and/or the editors, and should not be construed to be the views or opinions of the law firms or companies with whom such persons are in partnership with, associated with, or employed by, nor of the American Bar Association unless adopted pursuant to the bylaws of the Association.

Nothing contained in this book is to be considered as the rendering of legal advice for specific cases, and readers are responsible for obtaining such advice from their own legal counsel. This book and any forms and agreements herein are intended for educational and informational purposes only.

13 12 11 10   5 4 3

Library of Congress Cataloging-in-Publication Data

Tigar, Michael E.
    Nine Principles of Litigation—And Life.
    Michael E. Tigar
Library of Congress Cataloging-in-Publication Data is on file.

ISBN: 978-1-60442-400-3

Discounts are available for books ordered in bulk. Special consideration is given to state bars, CLE programs, and other bar-related organizations. Inquire at Book Publishing, ABA Publishing, American Bar Association, 321 North Clark Street, Chicago, Illinois 60654.

www.ababooks.org

Dedication

To E, J, J, K, and E—
for all of life's lessons

Table of Contents

Preface: Sources and the Litigator's Bookshelf ix

Chapter 1: Trial Lawyers Need
Principles of Life and Action 1

Losing Our Way and Finding It Again *1*

Principles in Action—A Story *5*

Principles in Action—How Would You ... ? *9*

Thinking about Others *13*

Counter-Narratives *16*

Sick and Tired: The Old Is Also New *17*

The Nine Principles *23*

Chapter 2: Courage 25

The Courage to Know Who You Are *27*

Zeal, Lawyers, and Jury Trial *39*

Courage and Clarence Darrow *46*

Courage to Say, "Let's Go to Trial" *49*

Courage to Stand Up to the Judge *55*

Courage to Confront the Jurors' Prejudice *63*

Courage to Stand Up to the Public and the Media
—and Your Colleagues *67*

Chapter 3: Rapport 89

Rapport with Your Client *89*

Rapport with Your Team *93*

Rapport with Witnesses *95*

Witnesses in My Favorite Movie *99*

Rapport with Judges *101*

Rapport with Jurors *105*

Chapter 4: Skepticism 121

Cynics and Skeptics *121*

Skepticism and Trust with Your Client *121*

Skepticism and the Human Condition *123*

Skepticism about Your Adversary *127*

Cultivating Skepticism among Jurors *132*

Telling the Judge to Be Skeptical *134*

Chapter 5: Observation 141

"Well Observed" *141*

Learning to Observe from Different Perspectives *146*

Using Others' Eyes and Ears—and Insights *149*

Ambiguity—for and against You *150*

Seen and Unseen Elements of the World around Us *152*

Helping Jurors to Observe *159*

Witnesses as Observers *161*

Chapter 6: Preparation 165

Say Your Case *165*

Preparation: Organizing Evidence and Exhibits *166*

Preparation for the Tasks of Trial *172*

Preparation for Arguing to Judges *175*

Chapter 7: Structure 181

Images of Structure *181*

Structure of Legal Rules *182*

Structure of Your Team *188*

Structure of Evidence Rules *193*

Structure of the Case Plan *194*

Structure of the Courtroom Space *199*

Structure of Opening Statement *201*

Structure of Direct Examination *213*

Structure of Cross-Examination *215*

Structure of Closing Argument *220*

Chapter 8: Candor 227

Your Candor *227*

The Other Side's Candor *232*

The Judge's Candor *237*

Your Client's Candor *240*

The Witness's Candor *241*

Chapter 9: Empowerment 245

The Experience of Being a Juror *245*

Transparency and Empowerment *248*

A Template for Empowerment: Expert Witness *251*

Don't Send Flowers, Plant Seeds *263*

Chapter 10: Presentation 267

Place of Presentation *267*

Dead Reckoning *271*

Exhibits: Presentation by Showing and Telling *274*

Presenting Witness Examination *276*

Markers, Tone, and Words *278*

Presenting Yourself *280*

Index 284

About the Author 289

Preface

Sources and the Litigator's Bookshelf

Although recycling is noble, and I have done some of it by reproducing portions of my earlier work and by making fair use of others' work, there must be limits. One limiting principle is avarice: I want you to buy my other books. Another is respect for literary property. A third consideration is my own belief that we become better lawyers by studying what other advocates have done and their views on how to endure litigation and life. Throughout this book, you will find references to the works on the list below. The books are available from Professional Education Group (proedgroup.com), the ABA (aba-books.org), Amazon.com, or your local bookstore, where they can look them up and order them for you. These books contain further detail on the topics discussed in this book. There are more specific references at the end of each chapter.

- Michael E. Tigar, *Examining Witnesses* (2d ed. 2002) (ABA Press)

- Michael E. Tigar, *Persuasion: The Litigator's Art* (1999) (ABA Press)

- Michael E. Tigar, *Fighting Injustice* (2002) (ABA Press)

- Michael E. Tigar, *Thinking About Terrorism: The Threat to Civil Liberties in Times of National Emergency* (2007) (ABA Press)

- *Trial Stories* (Michael E. Tigar & Angela Jordan Davis, eds. 2007) (Foundation Press)

- *Attorney for the Damned* (Arthur Weinberg ed. 1957)

- Terence MacCarthy, *MacCarthy on Cross-Examination* (2007) (ABA Press)

- Michael E. Tigar, *Opening Statement and Closing Argument* (Trial Phase), No. XXV in Classics of the Courtroom Series, Professional Education Group 1992)

- Michael E. Tigar & Jane B. Tigar, *Federal Appeals: Jurisdiction & Practice* (3d ed. 2000) (West)

- Michael E. Tigar, *Empowering the Jury* (16 DVDs, available from PEG)

- Michael E. Tigar, "Defending: an Essay." 74 *Tex. L. Rev.* 101 (1995)

- Michael E. Tigar, "The Power of Myth: Justice, Signs & Symbols in Criminal Trials," *Litigation*, Fall 1999, p. 25

Trial Lawyers Need Principles of Life and Action

Losing Our Way and Finding It Again

We are in danger of losing our way—to the courthouse, to justice, to principles of living that sustain us. By "we," I mean each of us individually, and as a profession devoted to helping people claim justice. We don't need doomsayers and preachers. We need principles of action, in litigation and in life, to keep us on the road, to get us out of the ditch, or to guide us back out of the thicket. The signs are all around us. Jury trials, hallmarks of the adversarial system that defines our image of justice, are on the wane. The rules of civil procedure have been amended in ways that increase the pressure to settle cases, fail to limit expensive and wasteful discovery, and make litigation more and more expensive. Inadequate representation and the pressure of sentencing guidelines are among the reasons why defendants waive their right to a trial.

When we do litigate, we are tempted to delegate important tasks of case control, and even the choice of stories and strategies, to consultants armed with sampling techniques and computer models. We forget to sit down and do the job for which we are supposed to be qualified—thinking through the case and how it should be tried. We often forget the simple truth that our job is to listen to, understand, and tell narratives about justice.

Even major corporations, sophisticated consumers of legal services, are sometimes ill-served by the counsel they hire. In case after case, one sees that litigation counsel treat cases in a routinized way, delegating tasks piecemeal while the case as a whole spins out of control. Then, if there is a trial, the failures of organization, of theme-building and team-building, become painfully clear. In this book, you will find examples of this sort of thing. Then, too, treating any case as simply routine—even in a busy practice—takes a lot of the fun out of practicing law, and that is another theme you will find in these pages.

As we read of young lawyer dissatisfaction with the profession, of poor people not having access to justice, of partner salaries heading toward the stratosphere while firms ignore the obligations of community service, we can see another method of losing one's way. Who are the lawyers whose example we should follow, and how did they unite ideas of life and of work?

I have therefore set out to write a book about trying cases, but along the way to conjure the images of trials and trial lawyers to suggest a way of living as well as of doing. In earlier writing, I have discussed the elements of trials: opening statement, direct examination, cross-examination, and so

Chapter One

on. I have stressed the need to empower jurors to see the case in a particular way, and the importance of having a coherent story. I have addressed the crisis of democratic governance, the challenges to our professional lives and livelihood, and have even shared some of my life experiences.

In this book, I want to unite these fields of thought. This is not a "lifestyle" book, nor a trial advocacy handbook. It is based on the idea that saying, "I try cases," means that one has decided that fair and open presentation of claims and defenses is not simply a good idea, but a way of living in the world. You will not, therefore, find detailed prescriptions about living. The great trial lawyers of this and all other times have defined themselves as seekers for justice. I therefore believe that if you seek out principles about how, why, and for whom to seek justice, that voyage will lead you to discover how to live your life. The nine principles that are chapter headings, and listed at the end of this introductory chapter, resonate in life as well as in litigation.

It may seem a bold claim that principles of litigation can also be those of life. Think about it. We like jurors who are open-minded. We want them to set aside their prejudices, to listen to both sides, to respect principles of justice, and to have the courage to give us a "ver-dict," literally, their "truth speaking." We hope they will not be tossed this way or that by the winds of public passion. We expect judges who listen carefully and rule without bias. In short, we want the rules of reason, justice, and compassion that we hope to find in our personal and professional lives to be at work in the arena where we have chosen to work. This book may convince you that this is so, but, if not, you at least may gain a few ideas about trying cases.

This book is for all trial lawyers. I draw on what I have already written and said. But this book is not "recycled material." I have taken ideas from times past and tried to burnish them in light of my own and my vicarious experience. I prefer the image of an upward spiral, passing over the same point but from a better perspective. When we think about the same old tasks from different perspectives, we gain new insights. The wise and skillful editor who took this manuscript in hand wondered if some, maybe most lawyers, have no need of a "fresh and creative approach to the practice." Oh, yes, they do, I would respond, and especially those who wonder if they do.

When I was a law student at Boalt Hall, the law review editor-in-chief several years ahead of me had joined a prominent Los Angeles law firm. Believing in the right of every person to legal representation, he accepted appointment as counsel in a criminal case. He rose to cross-examine the prosecution's leading witness, and realized that he did not know how to get the impeaching document into evidence before the jury. The jury found his client guilty. He then moved for a new trial, confessing his difficulty, on the basis that the client had received ineffective assistance of counsel. The trial court granted the motion. The law firm was not pleased, but they got over it.

This lawyer had the will to serve. He understood a basic principle about advocacy—accepting responsibility. That principle served him well beyond its application to trial practice. This lawyer simply lacked the skill to get the job done as he knew it should be done. In this book, I address both will and skill.

Principles in Action—A Story

Let me tell you the story of a story. As you read, put yourself in the position of lawyers called to defend this woman, accused of killing her husband. Imagine yourself in that community, in that time, about to face a jury of your neighbors. On Dec. 2, 1900, John Hossack of Warren County, Iowa, was killed in his bed by two blows to his head. One of these was with a sharp object that opened up a five-inch gash. The other was with a blunt object that crushed his skull. John's wife of thirty-three years, Margaret Hossack, was at home, as were five of the Hossacks' nine children. Margaret was charged with murder and went to trial in April 1901.

The evidence that Margaret Hossack killed John Hossack was strong. Almost everyone in the small community knew that John Hossack had for many years behaved violently toward his wife and children. In 1900, the community sentiment was also firmly that such matters should be kept "within the family." The all-male jury—most of whom were married—convicted Margaret Hossack of first-degree murder. The jury recommended "mercy," meaning life imprisonment instead of a death penalty. The defense won a new trial based on error in the jury instructions, the Iowa Supreme Court no doubt influenced by evidence that even if Mrs. Hossack had killed her husband there were perhaps good reasons why. The state retried Mrs. Hossack, but the defense won a change of venue. The jury was unable to reach a verdict and the Warren County Board of Supervisors voted that no more money would be spent on the case. Mrs. Hossack lived on for thirteen years with her family.

Susan Glaspell was a journalist who covered the first trial. In 1917 she published a short story titled "A Jury of Her Peers," about a farmer killed in his bed, whose wife was charged with the murder. She later wrote a play, *Trifles*, based on the story. The story and the play have spawned studies and comments by lawyers and law professors concerned with story-telling in trials and with the ways in which legal categories do or do not permit expression of claims for justice.

For this moment, however, imagine that you were called upon to represent Mrs. Hossack. In "real life," she was represented by two well-known defense counsel. A few hours' investigation would reveal that community sentiment was arrayed against Mrs. Hossack. She and her children had let people know how abusive and dangerous Mr. Hossack had been. There had been talk of divorce and splitting their assets. To the extent that people spoke of these events, it was with a sense that revealing such things in public was somehow shameful.

There is no sign in the literature of the Hossack case that the women's movement had reached that part of Iowa. There had been no organized effort to attack the stereotypes of woman's role. In the major cities, by contrast, women were campaigning for the vote, for the right to enter learned professions, and for other aspects of equality. Their leaders were being arrested for public demonstrations. In some instances, these struggles were linked to the temperance movement. In 1910, a few years after the Hossack case, temperance leader Carry Nation was arrested for using her axe to bust up the saloon at Washington, D.C.'s Union Station. The lawyers in those big cities, representing those women, had a different narrative to understand and tell.

Defense counsel for Mrs. Hossack would also look at Iowa criminal law in 1901. Murder was the unlawful killing of another with malice aforethought. First-degree murder had the additional elements of premeditation and deliberation. An intentional killing would be reduced to voluntary manslaughter if done in heat of passion arising from an adequate cause. At that time, past spousal abuse might well not have been considered adequate cause, and a delay in acting on provocation would in any case preclude a claim of voluntary manslaughter. The criminal law, it was said, did not like "brooders."

The law of self-defense was similarly unavailing. One had, then as now, the right to use deadly force to repel a threat of such force. The situation is looked at from the killer's viewpoint, taking the killer as a "reasonable man."

It would therefore be clear to defense counsel that the judge would probably not give a jury instruction that gave the options of manslaughter or self-defense. In the intervening years, lawyers and judges have reshaped the law of homicide and justification to take account of situations such as Mrs. Hossack's.

Suppose for a moment that the law had been different. Defense counsel would nonetheless confront male jurors who would be reluctant to accept such ideas. And if they heard from her and her defenders that she was a killer, and came in with a first-degree murder verdict, they might be less likely to vote for mercy.

The result was a trial in which witnesses and counsel talked around the tragedy of the Hossacks' life. Mrs. Hossack said she was awakened by a loud noise that she assumed in hindsight had been the first blow to her husband's head. She ran from the bedroom. Her team minimized evidence of hostility between her and her husband, in order not to lend support to a motive to kill.

If you put yourself in the position of those lawyers, you can see the choices that trial counsel is forced to make. We understand the client in order to help her; we have rapport. We are skeptical about what we hear because we know human frailty and that our version will be subject to challenge by the other side. We use our powers of observation and investigation. We prepare relentlessly. We understand the limits of law, procedure, and rules of evidence: the structure within which we work. We may seek to portray evidence as more or less important, but never sacrifice candor. We empower juries and judges to hear us, even to see the essential justice of our cause even when the structure of rules forces us to mute aspects of demonstrable truth; in *Hossack*, the appellate court saw matters fairly clearly and awarded a new trial less on the law than on some idea that such a result was just. The lawyers exercised the art of presentation. In this paragraph are eight of the nine principles on which this book is based. The ninth, and first in order, is courage: the courage of one's convictions, to take on a case like this and to work in a community hostile to our goal.

From 1901 forward, the stories of women abused by their partners were told again and again, with lawyers deploying the same nine principles. Today, we would see a different legal structure. Rules of evidence and procedure would permit introduction of expert evidence, to bridge a gap between the jurors' experience and attitudes and the accused's life and motivation. These cases, and the publicity around them, have helped to change social attitudes as well as the shape of criminal law.

Principles in Action—
How Would You ... ?

Mrs. Hossack, according to the prosecution, not only killed her husband, but violated a social compact about what women were supposed to do and endure. Her lawyers had to bridge the gap between what jurors "knew" they believed, and what they must accept in order to acquit her. Here is another, more recent, story that illustrates some of these ideas. In the September 2007 issue of the *ABA Journal*, several lawyers were asked how they would defend Osama bin Laden if he were captured and brought to face the indictments pending against him in New York. The magazine summarized my responses:

Having saved the life of convicted Oklahoma City bomber Terry Nichols, Tigar says he would draw on the lessons from that case.

First, he would assemble the same defense team. Next would be getting to know the client. "No lawyer should take a case [like this] without spending a lot of time with the client," Tigar says.

"It's not my case. It is his. I'd really need to understand everything about the social, psychological and historical context in which he grew up and acted," Tigar says.

"Here we have a man who, from a very early age, had anger against what he regarded as the colonial occupiers" of his homeland, he says. "It's the concept of *umma*, the Muslim community of believers. The concept that the U.S. occupied these territories made a number of people very angry.

"Three or four years ago it would have been very difficult to talk about this. But now, because of the Iraq war, which also has made more people angrier and drawn more people to the banner of Islam, we do have more to talk about."

And he would want to talk about those issues in front of a jury, not just a judge. "You always want a jury," he says.

"People are going to say, 'My goodness, the jurors are going to be prejudiced.' But I'd rather have 12 prejudiced people than just one."

Tigar also would push for a voir dire process similar to the one in the Nichols case, which, he notes, took approximately five weeks and involved the individual questioning of some 1,000 prospective jurors. "It's indispensable in a case like this because jurors are reluctant to talk about their attitudes."

Some may see the issues in a criminal case against bin Laden as involving a world foreign to a potential juror. But, Tigar explains, "the issues are no different than in any other case. The job of a lawyer is to address those issues."

Tigar says that point must be made right off the bat during opening statements. "Assuming this case is about Sept. 11, I'd start out by making a statement about the horror of that day, so all of us in the courtroom understand what happened and that we at the defense table agree that is what happened.

"We would remind the jury that the prosecution may very well play for them images that they have seen, sounds of horror that they have heard, and repeat all of the images in the mind to get them so worked up that they say, 'By golly, someone needs to be punished for this.'

"It is the defense task to provide this jury with as much evidence as we can muster as to what really happened, to the extent that it is relevant to the decision that the jury has to make."

Tigar says he would call psychologists and social historians to help the jury understand how attitudes like bin Laden's are formed. These defense experts also could negate the intent required to make some of the acts a crime.

"Many people who commit acts that the state regards as criminal do so because they are placed in positions where they feel that they had no choice. I have never met Osama bin Laden, but I have met people who are very, very committed to a certain ideal about social change.

"I have found that sometimes, on the issue of intentional violation of a known legal duty, that psychologists and social historians can help us understand why the state might not be able to meet its burden of proof on the intent element," Tigar explains.

Tigar also believes in maintaining courtroom decorum. "The danger in a case like this is that the circus part would come from the prosecutors who want the jurors to get worked up and emotional to the extent that they go beyond what they are there to decide," he adds.

And should the case proceed to a death penalty phase, Tigar says that he would bring up proportionality and political attitudes. That means, for example, talking about how U.S. government policy 20 years ago supported Islamic radicals in Afghanistan. "These folks were armed and financed by the CIA. What did we think was going to happen? And then, in terms of proportionality, how many Iraqi civilians have died? These are the questions we need to answer about proportionality."

Tigar also might argue to the jury that the killing needs to stop somewhere and that the bin Laden case might be the place. "In a trial of Osama bin Laden, a life verdict is a powerful message."

And no matter the outcome, Tigar says the U.S.

government must remember that the world would be watching.

"A case like this tests our commitment in a very important way. A trial of Osama bin Laden, like Nuremberg and others, says as much about the entity that does the trying as it does about the defendant. It represents the real test of the commitment to providing fair, just and transparent procedures, even to those perceived as terrible enemies. It is not only demanded by the Constitution, but by the international community."

Thinking about Others

You may look at these stories and wonder aloud what they have to do with your practice. You may say that the stories your clients tell are different from those I have just related. If that is your response, I hope you will read this book, because I believe you are mistaken. The American novelist Willa Cather reminded us that the basic struggles of each life are remarkably similar: "There are only two or three human stories, and they go on repeating themselves as fiercely as if they never happened before." Recently I published an essay in an ABA book entitled *Raise the Bar*, on changes in the legal profession. I was talking about legal services for poor people.

I pause here to note one comment from the pro bono survey, "Pro bono is worthless and a waste of time. It is also economically inefficient." That view has been expressed by those who say that the poor's legal problems are best handled by lawyers who only make $40,000 a year, and that wealthier, higher-paid lawyers who want to help should send money to legal services programs.

In answer to this concern, I wrote,

In sum, it is wrong and silly to imagine that poor people have special types of poor people problems that are not worth the time of big-time lawyers. Beyond this, such a view rests on the demonstrably false assumption, discussed above, that justice can be understood solely or mainly as a cost-benefit calculus of dollars.

Your client may be out of a job, harmed by a defective product, at risk of losing his business because of a meritless lawsuit, losing custody of children he loves, facing only a few days in jail that may mean being fired, or suffering from any of dozens of other perceived injustices that to him or her are as significant as a "big-time" case.

When I teach procedure to law students, mostly in the first year of law school, we soon encounter the cases about garnishment and attachment. We study the Supreme Court's decision in *Fuentes v. Shevin*, holding that Florida law was unconstitutional because it permitted her creditor, Firestone Company, to seize property without notice and the opportunity to be heard. The case involved a fairly routine conditional sales contract. In most such cases, there is little question that the debtor owes the money and the creditor has the right to take the goods. So, we ask, how much process is due Mrs.

Fuentes? What procedures must the creditor follow? Can a court clerk authorize seizure or must a neutral and detached magistrate sign the order? Should Mrs. Fuentes have the right to counsel if she cannot afford counsel?

Inevitably, the discussion drifts onward to a supposed cost-benefit analysis. Judicial process may well cost more than the stove is worth. Shouldn't the cost of making the procedure reliable bear some relationship to the financial stake involved and to the risk of a wrong decision? When students invoke these considerations, often based on readings about law and economics, it is time to talk about things that might be "worth less" but are "priceless."

Every trial lawyer knows some of these things. In a lawsuit about injuries, the jury may award money damages for loss of companionship, for pain and suffering, or, in appropriate cases, to punish the wrongdoer. We learn to tell juries that nothing can bring back a lost loved one, or go back in time and prevent pain, but that they should set a sum of money damages that in some sense is the equivalent of what has been lost or suffered. Every day in family courts, judges make decisions about custody of children, surely one of the most significant issues in a child's life. There is no financial calculus in these decisions, yet they are "worth" a great deal.

Taking account of this learning, students begin to see that the adversary system has value even when one cannot assign a dollar figure to a claim or defense. They begin to see that having such a system, accessible to all and fairly administered, is a hallmark of any society that claims to enforce justice. They then can move on in their learning, taking a critical stance toward particular failures of justice and systemic failures to see justice done.

It is not only the law students who need reminding. One task of the lawyer who takes those cases is to convince the tribunal that the matter is worthy of attention, and that must be done even before addressing the merits. The judges are not cruel, said G.K. Chesterton, they just get used to things. The lawyer who must battle for justice in a system that has cultivated indifference to the problems of daily life faces a special challenge.

Counter-Narratives

Reading the examples I have given, you may say to yourself, "Wait a minute. There are opposing stories to tell. Mrs. Hossack's husband lies dead and the law should do something about that. Osama bin Laden is responsible for thousands of deaths, and there should be a reckoning." You may say to yourself that you would rather prosecute Mrs. Hossack, or be a juror who votes a death penalty for Osama bin Laden.

The story, or narrative, is always mediated. One hopes that the adversary system operates under conditions of fairness and equality; if it does not, then one story may prevail simply because the side that tells it has an unfair advantage. Assuming parity, there are four limits to think about.

First, unless you are appointed by a court or are the last best hope of a client, you can usually decline a representation when the story that must be told for that client conflicts with your principles.

Second, when you think of a client's story, you must also consider the opposing story. Indeed, in real-life litigation, it is seldom that one version or the other will prove to be entirely right. A perceptive lawyer remarked that in ordinary litigation, "the debate is not so much between just and unjust, but correct or incorrect. There are respectable arguments on both sides, and no one could say that there would be any obvious injustice either way." That lawyer is mistaken. Most cases settle somewhere between the respective client positions. That locus of settlement is, or ought to be, determined by asking which view of justice has the better chance of prevailing, that is, which story has greater persuasive force. Every case calls forth the duty to think about justice.

Third, one is not free to invent any narrative that seems plausible. As later chapters show in detail, our narratives are bounded by ethical constraints, legal principles, procedural limitations, and rules of evidence.

Fourth, there are some principles that are, or ought to be, beyond debate. Torture and apartheid are always wrong. The Constitution guarantees certain rights that some of those who wrote it had earlier called "unalienable." A counter-narrative seeking to justify violation of these norms should be ruled out of order.

Sick and Tired: The Old Is Also New

As trial lawyers in the daily struggle to make a living, pay the rent, and keep the lights on, we ourselves sometimes forget these lessons. We are tempted to treat cases as part of a routine, instead of seeing each case and client as a new and exciting chance to help solve a problem. This malaise goes by various names—burnout, cynicism, even sloth. I had thought at one point to call this monograph COYOTE—acronym for Cast Off Your Old Tired Ethos, addressing the trial lawyer's malaise of falling into a routine. Eventually, I understood that COYOTE is too narrow an idea.

COYOTE has its uses, though. It can be used as a wake-up call. A couple of years ago, I was teaching at a seminar for lawyers appointed to represent defendants in capital cases. Many of these lawyers have been practicing criminal law for years, based in their home counties. I gave one talk on a Monday and was to give another on Tuesday morning. The seminar organizers and I were talking at breakfast on Tuesday morning. They remarked that many of the participants were resisting learning techniques of defense, saying things like, "well, I have been getting along just fine doing it this way," or, "that's not the way we do it in my county." They asked me to confront these attitudes as we began the day on Tuesday. So I used COYOTE as a battle-cry, a word that could be shouted out whenever somebody expressed a determination not to listen to a new or different idea.

> The teachers here have each tried capital cases, in many places and in front of many different judges and jurors. At the end of the day, you may or may not accept the ideas being suggested here. But listen. Capital cases are very different in so many ways, even from other cases involving serious crime. Your old ethos may not serve

you well, and the number of people on death row today tells us that some things need to change. Maybe some of those things are ways you approach your practice. Don't be afraid that you will be changed into something you are not. When the rain falls on an apple seed, it brings nourishment and a fuller, more robust apple tree. No matter how much it rains, that tree will still be apple and not mango.

COYOTE is an incomplete metaphor because the obstacles to doing justice involve more than the way that lawyers approach their work. Lawyers are advocates and counselors, but historically have also been public citizens with as much a duty as a right to participate in public affairs involving access to justice.

Of course, we often remind young lawyers that they cannot take on somebody else's persona. Jurors will quickly sense the artificiality of such a pretense. "Be yourself," the saying goes, "everybody else is already taken."

Still, this book is mainly about what we do about our cases and clients, and not a prescription for social change. This book is designed to bring together ideas about trying cases, but in the context of a lawyer life well and profitably lived.

We cannot be afraid to re-examine our ideas about law and life. As the reader already knows, I tell a lot of stories about the past. A law student once asked, and not unkindly, "What was it like to live in history?" The question misses two truths. First, the present is also history, and the pace of change has increased. Second, a sense of history locates us and the social and cultural ideas that govern how we live. As jurors, judges, and lawyers come to represent a broader spectrum of gender, color, and social condition, the arena within which we tell client narratives is being changed, and this is a part of "history." As our very ideas of human rights are influenced by movements for change that sweep across the world, the elements of narratives we understand and tell will shift.

Yet, our ways of seeing and telling are rooted in the historical past. The idea of uniting ideas about life, public expression, and a system for seeking justice is hardly new. As I described in *Persuasion: The Litigator's Art*, our basic techniques trace to Greek and Roman schools of rhetoric.

However, the classical teachers of rhetoric taught more than technique. Indeed, the person who pleads the causes of others has traditionally dwelt apart, possessing a set of values that define the profession. Sometimes, indeed too often, these values bespeak a claimed superiority, a guild mentality.

The Inns of Court, as they came to exist in fifteenth century England, were places for upper-class men, as Fortescue wrote in his famous book, *In Praise of the Laws of England*:

> There is in addition to the study of law a kind of academy of all the manners that the nobles learn. There they learn to sing and to practice all kinds of harmony. They are also taught there to dance and engage in pastimes that are proper for nobles.

But in most historical periods, eloquent voices have lamented the formalism that characterizes a profession that distances itself from common concerns. The great Latin advocate Cicero mocked the pretensions of lawyers in a famous trial speech, "Pro Murena."

The Roman author Petronius, who lived in the time of Emperor Nero, lamented that rhetoric teaching, and rhetoric itself, had become stylized:

> Is it not much the same type of madness that afflicts our declaimers, who shout: "These wounds I got, defending our common liberties; this eye I lost in your behalf. Give me a helping hand to lead me to my children, for my poor maimed limbs refuse to bear my weight." Even such extravagances might be borne, if they really served to guide beginners in the way of eloquence; but all pupils gain by these high-flown themes, these empty sounding phrases, is this, that on entering the forum they imagine themselves transported into a new and strange world.

> This is the reason, in my opinion, why young men grow up such blockheads in the schools, because they neither see nor hear one single thing connected with the usual circumstances of everyday life, nothing but stuff about pirates lurking on the seashore with fetters in their hands, tyrants issuing edicts to compel sons to cut off their own fathers' heads, oracles in times of pestilence commanding three virgins or more to be sacrificed to stay the plague,—honey-sweet, well-rounded sentences, words and facts alike as it were, besprinkled with poppy and sesame.

> Under such a training it is no more possible to

acquire good taste than it is not to stink, if you live in a kitchen. Give me leave to tell you that you rhetoricians are chiefly to blame for the ruin of Oratory, for with your silly, idle phrases, meant only to tickle the ears of an audience, you have enervated and deboshed the very substance of true eloquence.

Young men were not bound down to declamations in the days when Sophocles and Euripides found the very words they wanted to best express their meaning. No cloistered professor had as yet darkened men's intellects, when Pindar and the nine Lyric bards shrank from emulating the Homeric note. And not to cite poets exclusively,—I cannot see that either Plato or Demosthenes ever practised this sort of mental exercise. A noble, and so to say chaste, style is not overloaded with ornament, not turgid; its own natural beauty gives it elevation.

Then after a while this windy, extravagant deluge of words invaded Athens from Asia, and like a malignant star, blasting the minds of young men aiming at lofty ideals, instantly broke up all rules of art and struck eloquence dumb. Since that day who has reached the perfection of Thucydides, the glory of Hyperides? Nay! not a poem has been written of bright and wholesome complexion; but all, as if fed on the same unhealthy diet, have lacked stamina to attain old age. Painting moreover shared the same fate, after Egypt presumptuously invented a compendious method for that noble Art.

Or as Euripides wrote,

And avert thine eyes From the lore of the wise,
That have honour in proud men's sight.
The simple nameless herd of Humanity
Hath deeds and faith that are truth enough for me!

There is an Irish saying that gets at the same idea: If you listen to the river, you will catch a fish.

The Nine Principles

To express ideas about will and skill, litigation, and life, I have chosen nine principles. Each principle has subordinate parts, so the number could be greater; but that would make the format unwieldy. Or, the nine parts could be further combined to make five, or three. After all, we are told that the 613 commandments in the first five books of The Bible—variously the Torah and the Pentateuch, and also having a role in Islamic literature—can be summarized in the three-fold commandment in Micah 6:8 "to do justly, to love mercy and to walk humbly with your God." However, so sparse a number of principles could not logically deliver practical, workaday ideas about trying cases.

There is ample precedent for arbitrary numbering of principles. The "ten" commandments might be as few as nine, or as many as fourteen or fifteen. For me, the goal is to express values and ideas comprehensively, and yet in a way that permits the reader to focus on ideas that he or she finds most useful. The principles, each of which has a chapter of its own, are:

- **COURAGE**
- **RAPPORT**
- **SKEPTICISM**
- **OBSERVATION**
- **PREPARATION**
- **STRUCTURE**
- **CANDOR**
- **EMPOWERMENT**
- **PRESENTATION**

Note that presentation is last, preceded by eight princi-ples. A trial lawyer may find it odd that the actual perform-ance—the trial—occupies so little space. Think about it. Most cases are settled, so "preparing to present" describes most lawyer activity. And, as I will argue in different ways throughout this short book, a successful trial presentation is the culmination of careful and detailed work.

Notes

- On the troubled legal profession see *Raise the Bar: Real World Solutions for a Troubled Profession* (Lawrence Fox ed. 2007), which includes my essay, "The City Upon the Hill."

- The Hossack case is the subject of a brilliant book, Patricia Bryan and Thomas Wolf, *Midnight Assassin: A Murder in America's Heartland* (2007).

- *Law's Stories* (Peter Brooks & John Gewirtz eds. 1996) (contains valuable essays on which I have drawn for many ideas).

Courage

Some years ago, I reviewed a book on techniques of persuasion. I found the book empty, in the sense that it prescribed tactics without being concerned with a commitment to justice. I wrote, "In litigation as in love, technical proficiency without passion is not wholly satisfying." The remark was flippant and, as I look back at it, inadequate to express my intended meaning. I meant to capture the sense of daring and fortitude that all great trial lawyers exhibit. The seventeenth century English poet John Dryden satirized a political leader of his time, calling him:

> A daring pilot in extremity;
> Pleased with the danger, when the waves went high
> He sought the storms; but for a calm unfit … .

Yes, there is something of that adrenaline-seeking intensity-loving at the core of every trial lawyer's being. One is reminded of the old man in Samuel Beckett's play, saying:

> Perhaps my best years are gone … but I wouldn't want them back. Not with the fire in me now.

Fire, yes, but the fire of a stove or furnace, controlled and put to a good use, and not an uncontrolled conflagration. One is seeking Dryden's "daring," Beckett's "fire," and a capacity for calm reflection. For the first principle of nine, I have therefore chosen the word "courage." This word, in various connotations, describes an important value that trial lawyers must embody. We have all heard, and some use, the cliché, "courage of one's convictions." Yes, one must have courage to express a belief, and to confront hostile authority in doing so. But that use of courage assumes that one is already on a well-chosen path. What path? How to choose? Does the choice matter?

Last things first. The choice matters. Who are the lawyers whose example we would choose to follow? Which lawyers do we respect? If we make a list, we shall see that a commitment to justice distinguishes great lawyers, in their lives as in their work.

The courage you need is not simply to take on great causes against implacable foes. In our daily practice, we confront many barriers, some great and some smaller, to being effective and ethical advocates. It takes courage in our daily lives to confront these. Some time ago, there was a scandal in the U.S. Department of Justice. A lawyer I have known for many years emerged in the press coverage as a sort of hero, because he repeatedly told department employees to tell the truth and not to perpetuate a cover-up. In a telephone call, I congratulated him for his courage. He demurred, saying all he had done was tell people to follow the rules. I quoted to him the Russian dissident poet, Yevgeny Yevtushenko:

Chapter Two

How sharply our children will be ashamed
taking at last their vengeance for these horrors
remembering how in so strange a time
common integrity could look like courage.

The Courage to Know Who You Are

In 1988, I sat in the waiting room of a solicitor's office in Umtata, Transkei, South Africa. Transkei was one of the "homelands" established by the apartheid government where Africans could be "citizens." Transkei, Venda, Bophuthatswana, and Ciskei (the TVBC states) were simply artificial creations designed to enforce racial separation. The official publication of South African solicitors, a copy of which was in the waiting room, contained an editorial about apartheid. The editorial writer protested that lawyers should not be criticized for remaining silent in the face of apartheid, nor for helping their white clients take advantage of the benefits of that system. After all, the editorialist went on, lawyers should take the law as they find it. No wonder that the South African organized bar did so little to combat apartheid and in a post-apartheid world has continued to campaign for limits on access to justice.

This editorial should make us think about what it means to be a lawyer. I accept that sometimes we will provide our services in ways that lead to a result that seems unjust. The first requirement of courage is to know yourself, and to understand why you are doing what you have chosen to do.

Here is an excerpt from an essay I wrote several years ago, containing a tentative and partial approach to this issue:

Someone at a party asks you, "How can you represent a defendant you know is guilty, and then get them off?" Maybe adding, "… on a technicality?" You can give a little lecture on the constitutional right of counsel, or the government's heavy burden to prove guilt beyond a reasonable doubt by admissible and lawfully obtained evidence. You can repeat what [a Texas judge] said to a district attorney, "I see you quoted to the effect that my rulings on the constitutional issues were technicalities. I don't think of the Constitution as a technicality, and I hope you don't either." That won't placate your interlocutor, but it will blow enough smoke to let you escape to the hors d'oeuvres table or slip quietly away to your office to work on next week's capital trial.

Those answers will usually have to suffice, because we are forbidden in so many ways from telling our clients' secrets in order to justify our choices of causes and strategies. We are forbidden from expressing a personal belief in guilt or innocence. We risk crossing the lines of propriety when we say why we chose to accept a particular case, except of course to invoke the generalization that everyone is entitled to counsel and that this case raises issues that deserve to be well tried.

I am not saying that this rather formal justification of the right to counsel is trivial; the right to counsel is fundamental and worthy of defense. My point remains: If my taking a particular case requires me to make a public justification, then I put at risk the right of all hated clients to representation, for if I don't have such a good reason to take the next case, I have harmed that next client in the public's eye. I have represented many controversial clients, so I take a lot of criticism that I cannot really answer. That's the nature of what we do. This is so partly because the cases we do as lawyers are not about us. They are about our client's liberty or life, and our finest service may at times be to keep our mouths shut. ...

When you represent a demonized client, you may yourself be demonized. That is the risk you assumed by becoming a lawyer. Your defense is to rely on the bar's and your own independence, and not to relate unsavory allegations about your client and your relationship with him or her.

This is not to say that you will never share your private thoughts. Clarence Darrow said to juries, "I am not bound to believe them right in order to take their case, and you are not bound to believe them right in order to acquit them." When Atticus Finch summed up, and talked about the unthinkable idea that a white woman could desire a black man, he was revealing something about his own cultural conditioning.

I do believe that each of us must develop a personal set of ethical precepts, to guide us in the selection of clients, causes, and strategies. To say this is not trite: I have seen so many lawyers who turn inward after years at the bar and wonder whether all their effort has accomplished anything worthwhile. One day toward the end of his service on the Supreme Court, Justice William J. Brennan, Jr., and I were having lunch in his chambers. We were looking over transcripts of arguments that Edward Bennett Williams had made to the Court. Brennan was preparing his remarks for the dedication of the Williams Library at Georgetown.

"I look back at my own life," the Justice said, "and I ask myself what I really contributed to this world where we live." He was not joking; it was simply his own practical sense shining through. And of course the answer was and is that he contributed much. He was, as Justice Antonin Scalia said to some of us at Brennan's memorial service, "the most influential Justice of this century," and he then quickly added, "of course a lot of guys around here don't want to admit that."

I once was talking to a lawyer appointed to represent a 20-year-old man charged with capital murder for a drive-by shooting. In this jurisdiction, there is at least one charge of capital murder every week. This lawyer had looked at the discovery and interviewed the witnesses. He was convinced that he could attack the eyewitness identification of his client. We talked about strategy. Under the umbrella of privilege, he confided that he was convinced that his client had done the shooting.

He did not ask me what he should do. He had answered that question for himself, thoughtfully and honorably. He knew that his client had the right to have the line between guilt and innocence, life and death, drawn fairly and in a proceeding worthy of the name "justice." But I am asking you, the reader: What should he do? Don't send me your answer, because your answer is nobody's business but yours. If your answer does not include giving this defendant a vigorous defense, there is no shame in that. Just don't ever pretend that you would do that and then fail to do it. Don't take that case.

My answer, if I should be in such a case, is this: In that state and in that county, the legal system's switch has two positions, so far as the prosecutors are concerned: death penalty and acquittal. Bargaining in that case would be seen as weakness. Maybe on the eve of trial, if you keep in the game, you will get a plea offer, but only by continuing to show strength and resolve. I regard the death penalty as abhorrent under all circumstances, and an even more odious thing for a first offender with a troubled background. So I would represent this young man, first to give him what the Constitution commands, and second because I am comfortable with that moral choice and with the influence that his acquittal might have on prosecutorial discretion in future cases.

In November 2002 [the great Washington lawyer] Judah Best gave a talk entitled, "Would You Rather Do Direct Examination or Cross-Examination?" As I was writing this essay, I thought about his provocative title. The correct answer is "yes"—I would rather do direct and cross-examination, in a public trial before a judge sworn to be impartial and jurors fairly selected. "Rather than what?" you may ask. Rather than a secret military tribunal, rather than a secret immigration hearing with secret evidence, rather than all the compromises of the adversary system that are proposed every time this country's leaders get so scared that they lose confidence in constitutional government. ...

We uphold the right to counsel and all those trial rights not simply because constitutional government is a matter of our fighting faith. We uphold them because they work. Direct examination makes the story clear, one question at a time, each question and answer meeting the test of admissibility. Cross-examination tests the story told on direct. When government—or anybody with power—is free to hide behind truncated procedures, error abounds.

Justice Richard Goldstone [of the South African Constitutional Court and for a time Chief Prosecutor of the International Criminal Tribunal for Yugoslavia] reminded an audience at Yale of how the Nuremburg tribunal came to be. The United States insisted that a full, public, and fair trial of the Nazi leaders would serve a valuable didactic purpose. Judgments in historic cases, fairly tried, are safe from criticism from all but captious critics. Judgments in secret tribunals are inherently suspect.

In representing an unpopular defendant, or one who has concededly done great harm, you must choose a level of generalization at which you, the client, and the tribunal can meet. These days, we are seeing many cases in which the U.S. government seeks to substitute antiterrorist rhetoric for thought. If you are in a case like that, remind the judge of the ways in which the government has overstepped its lawful bounds and has been grossly inept or downright untruthful in this very type of case. You and the judge will, so you argue, have a shared responsibility to see that the rules are observed and the lines properly drawn. That is, if you are representing somebody accused of murder, your narrative is not about the social benefits of homicide but about the need for a fair hearing on culpability.

Our system of trials has the potential to be the most powerful engine for the discovery of truth. Wigmore said this of cross-examination, but he would more aptly have used the phrase to describe an entire system: adversaries equally matched, a fair and impartial tribunal, community participation, transparency and openness, vigorous advocacy, and—yes—direct and cross-examination. When the system fails to accord all of these rights, it is a pale and fraudulent imitation. A repressive government denying basic due process, and a bullying judge trying to shut off your cross-examination, are but different incarnations of the same iniquity, and you must have the courage to resist both of these.

We can test this assertion against many events in historical time. Behind the shield of secrecy and summary procedures have lurked official misconduct of all sorts. In the case of *Reynolds v. United States*, a famous journalist was killed when the Air Force plane in which he was riding crashed. His widow sued. The government convinced the Supreme Court that litigating the case would risk disclosing national security secrets about the airplane. Fifty years later, the relevant documents were declassified and it turned out that crash was due to a maintenance failure, and no secrets were involved. Learned Hand reminded us in *United States v. Coplon* that:

> Few weapons in the arsenal of freedom are more useful than the power to compel a government to disclose the evidence on which it seeks to forfeit the liberty of its citizens. All governments, democracies as well as autocracies, believe that those they seek to punish are guilty; the impediment of constitutional barriers are galling to all governments when they prevent the consummation of that just purpose. But those barriers were devised and are precious because they prevent that purpose and its pursuit from passing unchallenged by the accused, and unpurged by the alembic of public scrutiny and public criticism. A society which has come to wince at such exposure of the methods by which it seeks to impose its will upon its members, has already lost the feel of freedom and is on the path toward absolutism.

In 1999, a Los Alamos scientist named Wen Ho Lee was prosecuted for espionage-related offenses, and the government invoked secrecy to block revelation of the underlying evidence. After two years of litigation, it turned out that the prosecution was ill-founded, to say the least. Bumblers, bureaucrats, corporate wrongdoers, and government leaders intent on misleading the public fear the adversary system. Their fear is a testament to its power.

Beyond a broadly shared insistence on fair procedures,

and the courage to speak up, the trial lawyers whose work the profession celebrates have also shared a political ideology that values and promotes improvement in the human condition. I wrote some years ago in an essay about the Oklahoma City case:

> When I speak of a prosaic and down-to-earth idea of justice, I mean simply that one can deduce principles of right from human needs in the present time. That is, I reject the cynical, or Stoic, or no-ought-from-an-is idea that one set of rules is just as good as another. I reject the notion, as [the legal scholar and philosopher] Professor Martha Nussbaum has characterized it, "that to every argument some argument to a contradictory conclusion can be opposed; that arguments are in any case merely tools of influence, without any better sort of claim to our allegiance." Rather, again borrowing from Professor Nussbaum, my notions of justice "include a commitment, open-ended and revisable because grounded upon dialectical arguments that have their roots in experience, to a definite view of human flourishing and good human functioning." One element of such views is that "human beings have needs for things in the world: for political rights, for money and food and shelter, for respect and self-respect," and so on.

That is, so many great lawyers have shared the idea that justice requires more than fair procedures. If fair procedures are clockwork, one will still want to know what time it is. Martha Nussbaum is saying, and I agree, that providing for basic human needs is not simply a social preference, but rather a part of some verifiable idea of what justice truly means.

The idea that lawyers can, and perhaps should, have the courage to challenge authority and not accept the law as they find it, as that South African lawyers' magazine put it, has a respectable lineage. Indeed, one of the greatest lawyers of modern times wrote a seminal and powerful treatise on the matter. The young Dutch lawyer Hugo Grotius began to write about principles of justice in the early 1600s. His immediate objective was to argue for freedom of the seas, a concept that would benefit Dutch traders. He confronted a transnational legal regime whose basic principles were derived from "authoritative" statements by monarchs, the pope in Rome, and jurists who followed the path those rules had laid out.

For forty years, culminating in his work, "Of the Law of War and Peace," he formulated what some scholars have aptly called a "horizontal" view of justice, as distinct from the hierarchical, vertical view in fashion. Grotius believed that one could deduce principles of justice from social history, which is to say, human experience. He was, to be sure, a captive of the social and historical understanding of his time, and supported social ideas that are now regarded as unjust—such as slavery under certain conditions. However, his method of analysis has been adopted by movements for social change ever since. "Look around you at human suffering," advocates for change will say.

To take one example of what we might call the "Grotius method," consider the dispute over the death penalty in contemporary America. The debate over the death penalty can take place at a high level of abstraction, on moral and philosophical grounds. Supreme Court Justice Antonin Scalia is fond of putting the death penalty debate in terms of principles derived from legal, historical, and philosophical authority—that is, in vertical terms. Opponents of the death penalty point to the hundreds of innocent people who are convicted and sentenced to death, the lack of competent counsel, and the unfortunate tendency of police and prosecutors to withhold exculpatory evidence. We might call this idea of opposition "horizontal," as being derived from experience. Of course, opponents also make arguments based on "vertical" principles.

Challenging vertical thinking, the accepted ways of reasoning, takes courage. The great jurist Jerome Frank wrote that the law is not what it says but what it does. The courageous advocate will say to judges, "Before you tell me what the law is, listen while I tell you what it does."

To take another example, I once attended a seminar given by a law school professor who discussed whether a social host should be liable if a guest got drunk, drove negligently and injured or killed someone. This professor couched the debate in terms not only of the host's allegedly remote connection to the harm, but also of the drunken guest's "autonomy." By autonomy, he meant that the guest's decision to drink, get drunk, and drive represented a series of decisions that the guest made for himself. By giving the concept the name "autonomy," the professor was tapping into the accepted idea that people should be free to make their own decisions and should take the consequences. His argument was in the realm of vertically derived ideas about the role of people in society.

A horizontal approach would look at the number of deaths and injuries caused every year by people who abuse alcohol. It would note that a high percentage of people are genetically and environmentally predisposed to alcohol abuse; as to such people, the idea of autonomy is factually inapposite. After a couple of drinks at a party, almost everyone's judgment is somewhat impaired, clouding the decision whether to have "another one," or to get behind the wheel. If hosts were held liable more often, homeowners' insurance companies would put pressure on their insureds to monitor alcohol consumption. If hosts generally have insurance policies, the social costs of drunk driving would be spread.

There are two important reasons to understand the difference between vertical and horizontal justification. The first is that, by observing the world and its people, one can personally trace out the contours of justice. That is Martha Nussbaum's point about one's personal decision. That was Grotius' argument about the basis for sensible and just rules of conduct for his age.

The second reason has intimately to do with how we try jury cases. Jurors care about the law. For that reason, we take care in crafting jury instructions. We weave jury instructions into our closing argument. However, jurors do not hear the instructions until the evidence is in. All during the trial, they are hearing and seeing evidence and forming an opinion about it. They are using the sense of justice and injustice that they brought into the courtroom, and applying their life experiences to evaluating what they see and hear. In many, if not most, cases the jurors begin deliberation by asking themselves and one another how the case ought to come out, then tackling factual details and legal rules.

That is, jurors reason vertically—by paying attention to jury instructions—and horizontally—by applying their own experience and the experiences of those who testify. Most jurors want to do the right thing, which is always a combination of what the judge-given rules require and what their sense of right and wrong demands.

The great lawyers of this and all other recorded times understood the tension between vertical and horizontal ways of seeing problems in society and in the law. They had the courage that Grotius had, to challenge the given and accepted ways of viewing things. And they were better advocates for it.

Zeal, Lawyers, and Jury Trial

The English law of libel, as applied in the colonies and in the mother country, has many stories of lawyer courage. Prosecutions of dissenters for seditious libel were powerful weapons of the Crown. As Professor Thomas Emerson has said, "The English law of seditious libel prohibited any 'unjustified' criticism of government, its policies, or officials." The jury was officially permitted only to decide the fact of publication. The libelous tendency of the publication—the "innuendos" as they were called—was reserved to the judge. However, the jurors could by a general verdict of not guilty forestall the judge's power. And in 1670, the King's Bench had decided that jurors could not be punished for acquitting a defendant even if the judge thought the evidence was overwhelming.

Lawyers who represented libel defendants courted significant risks. Judges and other officials tended to lump them in with their clients as targets of obloquy or worse. If they mounted a vigorous defense, they might be held in contempt. We rightly celebrate the lawyers who showed courage in taking these risks.

Two examples, about two great advocates, illustrate the point. In 1735, the New York newspaper editor John Peter Zenger was charged with seditious libel, in that he wrote and published in his newspaper an article criticizing the colonial governor William Cosby. The grand jury refused to indict Zenger, so the prosecution proceeded by information. Zenger's New York lawyers moved to disqualify the presiding judges, Delancey and Philipse, because they served at the governor's pleasure and would not be impartial. For their impertinence in making this motion, the two lawyers— Alexander and Smith—were disbarred.

Alexander sent for Andrew Hamilton, a trial lawyer in Philadelphia, to come and try Zenger's case. Hamilton, then 68 years old, had compiled an enviable record at the bar and in public service. He had represented the Penn family and was a friend and associate of Benjamin Franklin. The verbal battle, with Hamilton on one side and the judges and attorney general on the other, was fought in the jury's presence. Quite early in the trial, Hamilton admitted that Zenger had published the papers in question. He then turned to two legal issues: the innuendos charged in the information and the truth of the alleged libels.

Zenger had written mockingly of the governor and his party, and Hamilton insisted that the jury had to decide whether the innuendos pleaded by the attorney general were supported by the proof. But his major verbal salvos were directed at the allegations that Zenger's paper was false, scandalous, and seditious. He first tried to persuade the judge that he could make the truth of the writing into a jury issue. When the judge ruled against him on that score, he turned to the jury:

> Then, gentlemen of the jury, it is to you we must now appeal, for witnesses to the truth of the facts we have offered, and are denied the liberty to prove; … I am warranted to apply to you both by law and reason. The law supposes you to be summoned out of the neighborhood where the fact is alleged to be committed; and the reason of your being taken out of the neighborhood is, because you are supposed to have the best knowledge of the fact that is to be tried. And were you to find a verdict against my client, you must take upon you to say, the papers referred to in the information, and which we acknowledge we printed and published, are false, scandalous and seditious; but of this I can have no apprehension. You are citizens of New York: you are really, what the law supposes you to be, honest and lawful men; and, according

to my brief, the facts which we offer to prove were not committed in a corner; they are notoriously known to be true; and therefore in your justice lies our safety.

Hamilton dared not openly urge the jurors to disregard what the judge had said. Rather, he turned to the old idea that jurors were thought to have personal knowledge of the dispute. This was indeed the law in England, but that last reported instance of jurors being witnesses was about 1550.

Hamilton then turned to his main theme:

All high things said … upon the side of power, will not be able to stop people's mouths when they feel themselves oppressed.

He continued in this vein:

To a generous mind, the loss of liberty is worse than death, yet we know there have been powerful men in all ages, who for the sake of preferment, or some imaginary honor, have freely lent a helping hand to oppress, nay to destroy, their country.

Power, you see, may be compared to a great river. If you keep it within its due bounds it is both beautiful and useful. But when it overflows its banks, it is then too impetuous to be stemmed. It bears down all before it, and brings destruction and desolation wherever it comes. If this is the nature of power, let us at least do our duty, and like wise men—who value freedom—use our utmost care to support liberty, the only bulwark against lawless power, which in all ages has sacrificed to its wild lust and boundless ambition, the blood of the best men that ever lived.

I am not equal to this undertaking. As you can see, I labor under the weight of many years, and am borne down with great infirmities of body. Yet old and weak as I am, I should think it my duty if required to go to the utmost part of the land, where my service could be of any use.

The question before you, gentlemen of the jury, is not of small or private concern. It is not the cause of the poor printer, nor of New York alone. No! It may in its consequence affect every freeman that lives under a British Government on the main of America. It is the best cause. It is the cause of liberty.

The jury acquitted Zenger, though both the attorney general and the chief justice told them their duty to find a guilty verdict was plain. Of the case, Declaration of Independence signer Gouverneur Morris said, "The Trial of Zenger in 1735 was the morning star of that liberty which subsequently revolutionized America."

On the other side of the Atlantic, later in the 1700s, English libel lawyers stood up to hostile judges, and in 1792 Parliament amended the libel law to expand jury sovereignty. Seditious libel was not dead—even Thomas Jefferson advocated its use against his political enemies—but it ceased to be such a ponderous weapon.

One notable advocate of press freedom was Thomas Erskine, a barrister who practiced in London from 1778 until be became Lord Chancellor in 1806. Erskine defended a number of dissidents, including Thomas Paine.

In 1784, Erskine represented D.W. Shipley, Dean of St. Asaph, who was accused of publishing a libelous pamphlet. The jury returned a verdict "Guilty of publishing only," arguably meaning that they did not accept that the pamphlet had the libelous tendency alleged in the indictment. Erskine demanded that the verdict be recorded exactly as given. Justice Buller insisted that "the verdict must be misunderstood."

Erskine: The jury do understand this verdict.

Justice Buller: Sir, I will not be interrupted!

Erskine: I stand here as an advocate of a brother citizen and I desire that the word "only" may be recorded.

Justice Buller: Sit down, sir! Remember your duty, or I shall be obliged to proceed in another manner.

Erskine: Your Lordship may proceed in what manner you think fit. I know my duty as well as your Lordship knows yours. I shall not alter my conduct.

Erskine took his seat in the House of Lords when elevated to the peerage and heard the evidence in the historic trial of Queen Caroline for adultery in 1820, in which her "peers" were the peers of the realm. In deliberations upon the evidence, Erskine famously remarked, "Proceedings of this kind, my lords, have never been tolerated save in the worst of times and have afterward not only been reversed but scandalized." He therefore proved that at the age of 70 he still possessed the gifts of advocacy that had sustained his practice.

Hamilton's and Erskine's lives and work reflect the synthesis of all the different kinds of courage that a trial lawyer needs. They were public citizens, using their law training to identify and combat injustice. They took on cases that might not win them friends in high places, and because they expressed values held by many of their fellow citizens they achieved success despite the risks they took. In trial, they were learned and fearless.

They knew that to represent a libel defendant one did not need to defend the content of the defendant's publication. To represent an alleged traitor did not mean to embrace treason. Rather, they could use their skill and learning to find a level of rhetorical abstraction on which the jurors' sense of justice would be engaged. That level of abstraction might be the quality of the prosecution's evidence and the requirement of proof beyond a reasonable doubt, or the unfortunate effects of sustaining the opponent's legal position.

Of course, there are many stories of trial lawyers facing hostile judges. Here are two of my favorites, which may be apocryphal:

> *English Judge (sitting in Ireland):* Mr. Curran, if you continue in this manner, I shall have no choice but to commit you for contempt.
>
> *John Philpott Curran:* Then your lordship and I will both have the satisfaction of knowing that it won't be the worst thing your lordship has ever committed.

And another:

Judge: Mr. Fallon, is that liquor I smell on your breath.

Mr. Fallon: If your honor's sense of justice is as good as his sense of smell, my client has nothing to worry about today.

These stories seem funny to me because I can imagine the circumstances, based on so many encounters with so many impatient and even hostile judges. Curran was an Irishman in colonial Ireland; the English judges were notoriously harsh on him and his colleagues. Fallon was one of those lawyers who confronted judges day in and day out in the busy criminal courts—the judges who "get used to things." Courage can be found in the day-to-day combat of litigation.

Courage and Clarence Darrow

No words of mine could or should compete with Darrow's autobiography, and with the collection of his words entitled *Attorney for the Damned.* Both books should be on every lawyer's shelf.

Darrow's jury speeches are a sterling example of seeking a point of contact between juror sentiment and case-winning issues. He dared juries to rise above their prejudices. Many of his cases involved homicide. In one case, an African-American, Dr. Ossian Sweet, was charged with murder for firing into a crowd of whites who were attacking his home. The legal issues were self-defense and defense of habitation. The defense of justification requires that jurors view the matter from the killer's point of view, assuming the killer to have been a reasonable person. As we saw in discussing the Hossack case, the reasonable person in Darrow's time was a white man of property. Darrow's struggle was to enlist jurors to put themselves in the client's place, to bridge the gap between their life experiences and his. In doing so, he laid out the history of racial injustice and enlisted jurors to do their part to correct it.

A second major theme in Darrow's cases, particularly those involving labor organizing, was the informer witness. The defendants in these cases were charged with organizing and using violence. Usually, the principal witness against them was someone who claimed to have been their accomplice, or had infiltrated their organization on behalf of the police or the employers. Darrow's jury speeches sweep over the history of organized labor, inviting jurors to share the life experiences of working people. He can then portray the informer as faithless—to his brothers and sisters as well as to his oath.

Darrow's background did not prepare him for these roles. He grew up in a tolerant household, but began his law career working for the railroad. Many biographers date his conversion to trial lawyering and representing underdogs to his 1894 defense of labor and political leader Eugene V. Debs. The story of his developing courage of his convictions begins earlier. He became interested in social issues in the late 1880s. He was convinced that the eight defendants convicted of bomb-throwing in the Haymarket trial of 1886 were in fact innocent and that their trial was a sham. He raised his concerns with Judge John P. Altgeld and, when Altgeld became

Illinois governor in 1892, urged Altgeld to pardon the three who had not been hanged and still survived.

Altgeld issued the pardon, making detailed findings of the trial's unfairness and the culpable role of public officials, including the judge, in causing this injustice. But Altgeld had warned Darrow that granting a pardon would be politically costly:

> Go tell your friends that when I am ready I will act. I don't know how I will act, but I will do what I think is right. We have been friends for a long time. You seem impatient; of course I know how you feel; I don't want to offend you or lose your friendship, but this responsibility is mine, and I shall shoulder it. I have not yet examined the record. I have no opinion about it. It is a big job. When I do examine it I will do what I believe to be right, no matter what that is. But don't deceive yourself: If I conclude to pardon those men it will not meet with the approval that you expect; let me tell you that from that day I will be a dead man.

For his own courage, Altgeld deserves a place in some pantheon or other. The poet Vachel Lindsay spoke of "Altgeld, brave as the truth, whose name the few still say with tears" and wrote a poetic eulogy on Altgeld's death.

The pardon, issued in 1893, must have helped move Darrow toward his decision to represent Debs and then to take up so many other causes—some fifty murder cases, for example, and in only one was the client executed. That case was the first one he tried, so there is something to be said for experience.

When Altgeld, as he predicted, failed in his re-election bid, Darrow made space for him in Darrow's law office. And at Altgeld's funeral in 1902, Darrow walked alongside the coach carrying Altgeld's body, and spoke an eloquent elegy to his friend. One senses that Darrow's own courage was molded in the example that Altgeld had set.

Courage to Say, "Let's Go to Trial"

I turn now to a more prosaic kind of courage. The courage to decline a settlement offer is not based on bravado, or ego. It is a practical decision about evidence, juror sentiment, and the power of a story. The trial lawyer makes the decision in a context. In the civil and criminal courtrooms across the country, formal and informal systems of docket control increasingly discountenance going to trial.

On the civil side of the docket, lawyers face increasing pressures to settle cases short of trial. Judges employ more case management techniques, including compulsory mediation, repeated case management conferences, and even threats of sanctions. Litigation increasingly involves complex issues on which expert testimony is necessary, which drives up case costs. Discovery battles are expensive. Repeat players, such as insurance companies, have devised formulas for settlement offers in most automobile and other ordinary tort cases. They play a take-it-or-leave-it game, and are willing to absorb an occasional jury verdict as part of their overall strategy.

I have known trial lawyers who become trial judges and

soon lose their enthusiasm for having cases tried. An experienced and talented trial lawyer who became a judge speaks now of managing a docket of 500 cases, and pressuring the parties to settle in order to relieve docket pressure.

Some of the blame for the decline in jury trials belongs with trial lawyers. Many lawyers do not investigate their cases before filing, and delay taking discovery even when the case is filed. Indeed, some lawyers file cases and then hold off serving the complaint in the hope of getting a settlement before the local rules require service to be completed. One judge to whom I spoke reported that the rule requiring service within sixty days was mostly not observed or enforced.

You cannot settle a case that you are not prepared to try. I don't mean that every witness and document is lined up. I mean that you must have enough command of the case that you could make a decent opening statement and a sketchy though well-organized closing argument. In the typical tort case where the defendant's insurance company is on the other side, the defendant will have had an investigator working, will have assembled relevant documents, and then put the information into an established matrix. A plaintiff who does not do an equivalent amount of work cannot make an informed decision on whether trial is a good idea.

On the criminal side of the docket, the pressure of sentencing guidelines, mandatory minimums, and the risk of a harsher sentence if the case goes to trial are significant deterrents to going to trial. However, the most significant negative factor is ineffective assistance of counsel.

In criminal courts all over the country, the spectacle of assembly-line guilty pleas and unprepared lawyers is acted out. Readers whose practice does not take them to criminal courts may be surprised at what goes on there. I wrote in a 2001 essay:

> The *National Law Journal* did a study of appointed counsel in capital cases in 1990. Given what is at stake, one would expect that only the most-qualified lawyers would be found adequate to the task. By now, almost everyone has read the anecdotal evidence that this is not so. The classic story of the Texas appointed lawyer who slept during his client's capital murder trial has made the rounds. The trial and penalty phase lasted just 13 hours, and the lawyer did not even make objection when the prosecutor said the jurors should sentence the defendant to death because he is gay.
>
> Here is a short summary of what the *National Law Journal* found:
> - "the trial lawyers who represented death row inmates in the six states were disbarred, suspended, or otherwise disciplined at a rate three to forty-six times the discipline rates for lawyers in those states"
> - "there were wholly unrealistic statutory fee limits on defense representation"
> - "nonexistent standards for appointment of counsel"
> - "capital trials that were completed in one to two

days, in contrast to two-week or two-month long trials in some states … where indigent defense systems were operating"

In short, the right to effective counsel is ignored in the cases where the stakes are highest, and error rates are demonstrably high. The idea that a capital case can be well-tried in one or two days is laughable. In the Oklahoma City bombing trial of Terry Nichols, jury selection alone took five weeks in order to get a panel that was willing to swear it could overcome the media barrage. The trial itself took nearly three months. The defense called more than 100 witnesses. The jury acquitted Nichols of murder, finding him guilty of lesser charges, and voted not to impose a death penalty. This result was achieved only because counsel had the dedication and resources to combat the government.

In non-capital cases, the situation is every bit as bleak. In April 2001 *The New York Times* published the results of a long investigation into the provision and performance of appointed counsel in New York City. It found that appointed counsel are paid at rates that actively discourage them from spending enough time on cases. The only way to make the appointed practice pay is by taking on hundreds of cases per year and spending as little time as possible on each one. The *Times*' "poster lawyer" was one Sean Sullivan. Sullivan handles 1,600 cases per year, and earned more than $125,000 in 2000 for his efforts. The "representation" he provides is worse than minimal. He does not confer with clients, does not return client phone calls, does not prepare needed legal motions, and contents himself with working out quick plea bargains on an assembly-line basis.

Civil and criminal lawyers need that "let's go to trial" courage. They need it for particular clients. They need it for their own reputations, for their clients, and even for the system itself. My friend and trial colleague Ron Woods—imagine a trial team called "Tigar Woods"—used the expression "dump-truck lawyers" to refer to habitual plea bargainers. If you have a reputation as a dump-truck lawyer, the adversary will make offers knowing that eventually you will cave in and settle short of trial. If you go to trial in good cases, and win a few because you have followed all the principles in this book, your presence in the case will bring better offers.

As for effect on the system, consider this: If you litigate against repeat players such as prosecutors, insurance companies, or individual lawyers who regularly appear in court, going to trial reveals information about tactics and techniques. For example, there may be a favorite expert that your adversary uses. This learning benefits you the next time out. It also benefits other lawyers and even judges—the adversary system sheds light, and reveals the strengths and weaknesses of party positions for all to see.

The litigation over the Merck drug Vioxx gives an example of why "let's go to trial" courage makes sense. Merck marketed Vioxx as a pain-relief drug beginning in 1999. On Sept. 30, 2004, faced with mounting criticism that the drug caused blood clots, heart attacks and strokes, Merck withdrew Vioxx from the market. The company then faced more than 10,000 lawsuits. Merck announced it would fight lawsuits one at a time, a strategy that carried great risk and expense. Merck's general counsel, Ken Frazier, was a seasoned litigator and he made the decision.

Leading plaintiffs' lawyers formed a consortium to share discovery and expertise. A federal judge put the federal cases into a multidistrict litigation (MDL) docket. The trials began. Merck won some. Plaintiffs won some. The trials illuminated the key issues better than any settlement negotiations ever could. They showed what different jurors' sense of justice and injustice—in different parts of the country—would play out in verdicts. They showed which legal theories might find favor with judges.

In short, the courage to say, "let's go to trial," established a meaningful market for the value of Vioxx-related claims, and helped promote a global settlement. The point can be generalized. Without well-chosen trials, there is no reliable benchmark for how cases "ought" to settle. In most cases, the parties want a settlement, and most cases should be settled. Settlements happen most readily when parties are ready to try their cases effectively, and show that they are not afraid to do so. Settlements are best when they are as demonstrably fair as possible, and that demonstration is best made by comparison with actual results.

Courage to Stand Up to the Judge

Erskine, confronting Judge Buller, had it easy. The jurors had voted. He wanted to uphold their evident intent. The judge was standing in the way. The tactic of confrontation was an obvious choice. The choice is not so easy most of the time.

Every trial is a dynamic process. The relationships within the well of the courtroom are many and complex. You have chosen jurors in the hope that the process of receiving and then deliberating on the evidence and argument will favor your position. For that reason, you may have challenged the very strong juror who you feel would have dominated the jury room discussion. You may have challenged one of a pair of jurors who know each other or who share certain views, for that combination of two jurors will become one voting bloc.

You know your adversary's personality, style of argument and objection. You understand how the judge wants to run his or her courtroom. You are even alert to the many, perhaps subtle, ways that other court personnel can influence the courtroom atmosphere.

You do not make a decision to confront the judge in the abstract, but in the context of the particular trial dynamic you are seeking to create and maintain. Some lawyers make a point of needling the judge. They seem to feel that their tactics will invariably create sympathy for them or their client, or distract the jurors from unpleasant facts. On the other hand, some say that no lawyer or party should ever show disrespect to the judge; they preach the gospel of "orderly trials," ignoring the history of judges who abused their power.

The courage to confront the judge is not a matter of gratifying one's own ego, and yet I hear lawyers boastfully say, "Well, I really told him!" In a jury trial, jurors often come into court with the idea that they must respect the judge. Judges play to this feeling, and assert their control through a variety of devices. They tell the jurors that what the lawyers say is not evidence. They repeat that the jurors must accept the law as given by the judge, disregard matter ordered stricken, not speculate what would have been the answer to an objectionable question, and so on. In a long trial, the judge may take special care that the jurors have refreshments in the jury room, and tell them kindly that he or she is making arrangements. In a high-profile case, where jurors may be escorted to and from the courthouse, they learn to depend on the judge and on court personnel for their peace of mind or even their safety. Few judges engage in ex parte communication with jurors, although there have been cases of that. The bailiffs or marshals are more likely to engage in that sort of conduct.

You, the advocate, on the other hand, need to establish your control of the courtroom. You insist that the judge listen respectfully to you. You show your command of the facts and the legal principles. You are entitled to try the case you have well-prepared and to present the story you have crafted.

When the judge's behavior gets in the way of these goals, that is the time to exercise your courage. These goals are not only permissible; it is your obligation to pursue them to the full limits of the adversary system. When the judge is considering admitting an item of evidence that you believe is inadmissible and harmful, your duty is clear. Make an objection. If there is time, file a memorandum. Protect the record at all costs and all hazards. Some judges actively try to prevent counsel from making cogent objections on the record.

The judge may display impatience, condescension, even anger at objecting counsel. Before trial, you will have studied the judge and found out his or her habits in the contested evidence situation. You cannot exercise the courage to object unless you have first understood the objection options under the rules of evidence and made a conscious decision to object rather than let the matter go. It may be that you are willing to have some evidence come in because it opens a door you want to walk through later.

Having decided to object, and having lost, your job is not necessarily done. You may be able to seek a limiting instruction—not admitted for the truth of the matter, admitted for a limited purpose, and so on.

There are many other times at trial when the judge's conduct will require an objection. A notable example from California tells a story of courage in the face of a hostile judge.

In 1960, the well-known California lawyer Grant Cooper was representing a man charged with killing his wife. A codefendant was charged as an accessory and was separately represented. The first trial had resulted in a hung jury and mistrial. On retrial, the jury had been deliberating for more than a week. The jurors had returned to court to ask questions of the judge. The judge answered the questions and expressed hope that the jurors would reach a verdict. Cooper objected to this comment as coercive and moved for a mistrial. The judge denied the motion.

More than week later, after the jurors had still not reached a verdict, the judge called the jury back into the courtroom. He stationed bailiffs behind each of the defendants even though this show of force had not been done before. The judge then began to comment on the relative credibility of the defense and prosecution witnesses, supporting the prosecution's case and casting doubt on the defense testimony. The judge had not told counsel he was planning to comment on the evidence, and had not reviewed his comments with defense counsel.

Just after the adverse comments on his client's credibility, Grant Cooper spoke up:

Mr. Cooper: If Your Honor please.

The Court: Now Mr. Cooper, I don't want a word out of you.

Mr. Cooper: If Your Honor please, as a lawyer I have a right to address this court.

The Court: You don't have a right to say a word when the jury is down here in the process of their deliberations, and I instruct you and Mr. Bringgold [counsel for co-defendant] to keep seated and wait until the jury is out to make your objections.

Mr. Cooper: If Your Honor please, I feel Your Honor has no right to invade the province of the jury.

The Court: Mr. Cooper, I hold you directly in contempt.

Mr. Cooper: Very well, Your Honor.

The Court: I will dispose of the matter as soon as
I have instructed this jury.

Mr. Cooper: Very well, if Your Honor please, it is
Your Honor's prerogative.

The Court: It certainly is, and I am going to exercise it.

As the jury was about to leave the courtroom, the judge
returned to the contempt theme:

The Court: One thing more before you go, you should
not in any way consider in your deliberations the fact
that the Court felt it necessary to hold Mr. Cooper in
contempt. That has nothing to do with the issues in
this case, and it should not be considered by you at
all. That is all.

Mr. Cooper: Now, if Your Honor please.

The Court: Just a minute, Mr. Cooper.

Mr. Cooper: I have a right to address the Court.

The Court: You do not; while the jury is here you do
not have any such right; you sit down.

Mr. Cooper: If Your Honor please, I feel Your Honor
has invaded the province of the jury.

The Court: That is a matter of subsequent argument; I
again hold you in contempt, Mr. Cooper. You sit down,
and then I will let you say what you want to say. You have
no business saying anything in the presence of this jury.

The California Supreme Court annulled the contempt citations, and the $250 fines the judge imposed, stressing its duty to maintain "an independent bar." When I was growing up in Southern California, Grant Cooper was perhaps the best known of the high-profile criminal defense lawyers. On his appeal to the California Supreme Court, he was represented by two other icons of the trial bar, Joe Ball and Herman Selvin.

The courage that Cooper displayed is an essential part of the trial lawyer's armory. Something is happening in the courtroom. It is wrong and harmful. Unless counsel objects, any reviewing court will hold the point to have been waived. The advocate risks the judge's ire by objecting. Perhaps the jurors have learned to respect the judge so much that in their eyes, the objecting lawyer comes off looking bad.

So far as one can tell, the trial judge's conduct in trying to get a guilty verdict in Cooper's case was an isolated event in a long trial. Sometimes, however, the judge's pattern of unfair conduct begins early and continues. In such a case, the lawyer must carefully weigh the risks of irreparably offending jurors by making a fuss.

First rule: Know the judge. Know that judge's style before you get into the courtroom, either by regular practice or by asking around. Second, develop a strategy. You should ask for a pretrial jury instruction that stresses the lawyer's duty to object as well as the judge's duty to rule. Develop a way of objecting: say, "Objection, Your Honor," rather than, "I object." Ask to be heard at sidebar, at the bench, or at a recess to make your record. Write short motions on contested points and pepper the judge with them; confrontations in writing are not for the jurors' ears. In closing argument, get right to it:

> You the jurors have a power like that of the ancient kings. This case is too important to be decided by lawyers, too important to be decided by the judge. You are the sole judges of the facts and nothing the judge, or any lawyer, says can take away from that.

These forms of confrontation may, at some point, lead you to be in Erskine's or Grant Cooper's position. You will have two solaces. First, the law on advocacy and contempt is on your side; appellate relief will likely arrive. Second, you will have shown a quality for which we celebrate those great advocates.

Some lawyers have confronted judges in high-profile trials, been held in contempt and seen the contempt citations affirmed. These cases fall into three categories. First are those in which the lawyer has been foolishly, willfully, and needlessly obstructive. I have known and seen professional "judge-baiters."

Second are cases in which the lawyer was laboring within an unjust system and acted in knowledge that punishment would probably follow but wanted to use that punishment to make a point. In apartheid South Africa, Godfrey Pitje, a courageous lawyer who practiced law with Nelson Mandela and Oliver Tambo, refused to sit in the courtroom seat set aside for Blacks. He was repeatedly held in contempt and punished. He was taking a necessary stand. Sometimes in trials the intended audience of words and action lies beyond the courtroom. Godfrey Pitje was addressing his words and conduct to the growing anti-apartheid resistance.

The third category is more difficult to describe and evaluate. For example, in some celebrated political trials, the lawyers—and sometimes also the defendants—have confronted the trial judge with anger. Their remarks have sometimes interrupted and slowed down the trial process. Bar groups hasten to condemn the lawyers' outbursts. Yet, with the advantage of historical hindsight, I sometimes find it difficult to see why the lawyers should have been punished.

In the 1969-1970 trial of activists for conspiring to encourage rioting at the 1968 Democratic Party convention in Chicago, defense lawyer William Kunstler was held in contempt for arguments and objections to Judge Julius Hoffman's trial rulings. I have reread the court of appeals opinion upholding some of those contempt citations, and reversing most of them. If one reads contemporary accounts of that unfair trial and how it came to be, and studies the outrageous conduct of the presiding judge, Julius Hoffman, one wonders how Kunstler could avoid becoming angry and concerned enough to strike back as he did. The obligation to obey the law rests upon an understanding that the law is being reasonably administered in a nondiscriminatory way. When the administration of what calls itself "justice" is demonstrably flawed, the system should be willing to accommodate a range of protest.

Courage to Confront the Jurors' Prejudice

Voir dire is the first opportunity to confront juror attitudes. Ideally, the jurors will fill out a questionnaire with basic information and answers about employment and such things as what they read and watch. From questionnaire answers and some basic understanding of community demographics you get an initial idea about prejudices that can affect your case. You may have juror addresses, and public information about their political positions, such as what petitions for office-holders and public issues they have signed. In your jurisdiction it may be permissible to drive by jurors' houses, discreetly, looking for car bumper stickers and yard signs and other indicators.

When voir dire begins, you will want to emphasize that truthful answers are always good even if the juror thinks somebody will be offended.

> Members of the jury, this is who I am. Now it is everyone's god-given right to be prejudiced. I have prejudices, biases, attitudes. I have just plain made up my mind about some things. Every person here will be a great juror, but maybe you have an idea about the issues in this case that would mean you would be a better juror for some other case in the courthouse.

Then a juror lobs one back at you. "Well, I think that these people that sue their employer over some workplace remarks are too thin-skinned." And there you are, with a juror prejudice and your client an employee in a wrongful termination case.

Have courage. You don't want to "blow the panel," that is, pollute the whole jury pool. You need to confront this situation.

> *You:* Thank you very much for that answer. I really appreciate your being straight with us. In this case, one of the things we will be talking about is the insulting and demeaning language used against Mrs. Wilson. The judge will tell you what the law is about that, and of course there will be evidence about what was said and who said it and why. I wonder if any jurors feel that if our law protects people against this kind of treatment, that is a good thing?

Despite good voir dire, jury selection is usually more "juror deselection." We can use the process to eliminate, for cause or by peremptory challenge, the jurors we feel are most negative. The other side is doing the same thing from its point of view. In many if not most cases, one or more jurors who wind up being selected will have attitudes of skepticism toward our case. Issues of politics, race, or religion may lie just below the surface. Attitudes toward plaintiffs claiming injury, insurance companies, plaintiffs' lawyers, lawyers in general. There may be community attitudes toward our client, or the kind of claim we are presenting or defending. We have all seen these in action. We are stuck with these twelve, or six, jurors. How shall we behave?

With courage, I say. In a play I wrote with Kevin

McCarthy based on real-life Irish lawyers, we used these words of Dan O'Connell, a great nineteenth century Irish barrister. When he was at the bar, Catholics such as himself were not eligible for public office. Jurors were taken from among those who had approved of the laws uniting England and Ireland and therefore upholding the English state church's dominant role in a country where most people were raised Roman Catholic.

> God bless England! She set over us Protestant judges and ruled that only Protestants, supporters of the Union with England, could serve on the juries. Oh, that was a challenge to the Catholic advocate. I learned to walk up to the twelve in the jury box and put it to them squarely.
>
> "This is not the time to discuss how you were put in that jury box, let alone get any remedy on that subject. There is considerable discrepancy of opinion between you and me, at least as to the Repeal of the Union. If you had not so differed from my own opinion, you would not be in this very box. This is a disadvantage which does not terrify me. You swore an oath to administer justice. I challenge you to keep it. Or will you let this prosecutor trap you into betrayal of your jurors' oath out of misguided zeal for your religion?"

As noted above, Clarence Darrow often approached jurors with a similar line of argument. In a more modern vein, here are two excerpts from an article I wrote in 1988. In the first excerpt, imagine an advocate who suspects possible juror prejudice, and decides to confront it. The method of confrontation is not to lecture the jurors, but to empower one or more of them to have their own courage—the courage to confront prejudice in the jury room.

Fidelity to the law—a rule-oriented argument—suits the advocate who is seeking to override prejudice that may lurk in the facts of the case. The jury may look upon the criminal defendant as a worthless bum, but "the law" bestows rights upon him and duties upon a jury, namely, to weigh the evidence.

"Suppose you are in the jury room, and somebody looks at you and says, 'Well, you know, that defendant didn't take the stand.' What can you say to that person? You can look them in the eye and say, 'Now wait a minute. We all took an oath that we would follow the law as the judge gave it to us. And the judge said, just as clear as anything, that the prosecutor has the whole burden of proof and the defendant doesn't have to prove anything. You can't hold it against the defendant that his lawyer advised him that this jury was made up of honest people who would follow the law the way the judge laid it out.'"

The second excerpt draws on the idea that jurors respect the oaths they took:

The law includes the obligations of the juror's oath. Every juror is examined, in voir dire, under oath. The oath will be more or less significant, depending upon how extensive voir dire has been. Every juror also takes an oath to try the case "well and truly." These oaths are rituals that the advocate must reinvoke in final argument.

"We all take an oath to be able to play our part in this case. I took one to be a lawyer. So did this prosecutor over here. His Honor took an oath, and swore to uphold the Constitution. This is the same oath that every judge across this land must take.

"And each of you took an oath. In fact, you took two. Just before the first witness came in to take the stand, you swore to well and truly try this case. And, I believed you then. When the lawyers and the judge were asking questions in the first part of the case, when we were choosing you to be jurors, you were answering under oath. You said that if this prosecutor did not prove this case beyond a reasonable doubt, you would vote 'not guilty.' And, I believed you then. You said you understood that in America somebody like Mr. Smith here, who is on trial for his liberty, does not have to prove anything. And, I believed you then."

Courage to Stand Up to the Public and the Media—and Your Colleagues

The media's role in the trial process can be troubling. For a lawyer in a high-profile case, the media's invitations to give an interview, make a comment, or appear on a television show can be beguiling. Where does courage come in? I think that the issues are best seen by first examining the constructive role that the media and lawyer comment have played in our history, and the First Amendment rights of trial observers and participants. Then, one can analyze the malign influence of media frenzy on trial fairness, particularly to defendants. From there, one can think about the prudent and courageous course for a lawyer. That is, you may have a defensible right to speak to the media, but wisely choose not to exercise it— for your client's sake.

It takes courage to refuse media attention, to take your case to the media as a means of seeking justice, to speak to the media to confront public prejudice against your client, and to face down a judge who thinks you have no business talking to the media at all. The public, and your law partners, may be troubled by your choice of clients. You need more than courage, however. And so you will find below some thoughts on how your courage might be deployed. Powerful forces are at work, some of which believe one should speak truth to power, and others who are will endeavor to speak power to truth.

Courage is often not enough. During the Civil War, a group of Quakers in Loudoun County, Va., decided that their antislavery and pro-Union sentiments should outweigh their pacifist beliefs. They courageously armed themselves to battle a Confederate detachment. They were almost all killed.

In colonial America, the lawyers who stood up against the Crown and for colonists' rights knew the power of publicity for their efforts. In the 1760s, John Adams was one of the lawyers for those resisting the unlawful arbitrary searches being conducted at the Crown's bidding. The colonist clients filed lawsuits challenging the Crown's powers. Adams acknowledged his role in publicizing those legal battles, and called attention to the positive effect of that publicity in building support for independence.

Here is another story, taken from my book, *Thinking About Terrorism*. It tells of a federal judge whom Thomas Jefferson's attorney general attempted to discredit by a media campaign against a decision Jefferson did not like:

> In 1807, Congress authorized an embargo on foreign seaborne commerce, as a measure of retaliation against British and French interests. The embargo was controversial, and it caused great hardship to commercial interests on the Eastern seaboard. It did not have the desired political effect, and on the domestic scene caused Thomas Jefferson's party to lose a great deal of political support. However, having been authorized by the Congress, it was held constitutional. Seafarers resorted to evasion and smuggling. One Congressional response was a statute of 1808 that permitted the federal customs collector of each port to detain any ship ostensibly bound for a domestic port whenever in his opinion the ship was actually headed to a foreign destination. The statute seemed to repose unfettered discretion in the executive branch.
>
> Enter Justice William Johnson, who was Jefferson's first Supreme Court nominee. Johnson, a well-respected South Carolina lawyer and judge, took his seat on the Court in 1804. As was the custom at that time, he sat as a trial judge "on circuit," and in that capacity, heard a

challenge lodged by a ship owner who had been refused clearance to leave the port of Charleston. The owner, Adam Gilchrist, claimed that his ship was bound for Baltimore, and was laden with rice and cotton. The collector of customs apparently suspected that the ship was really headed overseas.

Justice Johnson heard evidence and, with a written opinion, issued a writ of mandamus on May 28, 1808, directing the collector to clear the ship. Justice Johnson held that the courts had the power to construe the Congressional grant of power and to keep executive actions within lawful bounds. His language was polite, but his message was clear.

Jefferson, hearing of the decision, was angry. He asked Attorney General Caesar Rodney to draft a letter evaluating Justice Johnson's decision. Rodney complied, and among other arguments said that the court lacked jurisdiction because the Congress had given the President unreviewable power over the issue of port clearances, and that the President had exercised that power in telling collectors not to clear any vessels carrying certain kinds of cargo even though there was evidence the cargo was bound for a domestic port. Jefferson had in effect ordered that ships carrying certain foodstuffs and other articles that would logically be shipped abroad should be kept in port, regardless of their stated destination.

Upon receiving Rodney's letter, Jefferson authorized it to be published, and it appeared in a Charleston newspaper in the summer of 1808. Justice Johnson was appalled at Rodney's misstatements of fact and law, and at Jefferson's having had the letter published. He knew both men well, and professed his respect for them. However, he wrote a reply and then waited a few weeks before releasing it for publication. The reply stands as an important document in the history of judicial review, and as a cogent assertion of the role of judges in the constitutional system. Johnson began by saying that he would not have replied to a newspaper editor's criticism of his opinion. Editors have an unlimited right to comment. He went on:

> The official acts of men in office are proper subjects for newspaper remarks. The opinion that cannot withstand a free and candid investigation must be erroneous. It is true that a judge may, without vanity, entertain a doubt of the competency of some of the editors of newspapers to discuss a difficult legal question; yet no editorial or anonymous animadversions, however they may have been characterized by illiberality or ignorance, should ever have induced me to intrude these observations upon the public. But when a bias is attempted to be given to public opinion by the overbearing influence of high office, and the reputation of ability and information, the ground is changed; and to be silent could only result from being borne down by weight of reasoning or awed by power.

The Justice Johnson story is two centuries old. Yet one can find many more recent examples of official efforts to intimidate judges who take principled positions.

There are many instances of media attention being focused on legal issues in a constructive way. I was briefly involved in the defense of Freddie Pitts and Wilbert Lee, sentenced to death in Florida for allegedly killing a gas station attendant during a robbery. *Miami Herald* reporter Gene Miller investigated the case, helped find the real perpetrator of the crime and also the coercion exercised against Pitts and Lee in jail. The stories of innocent men and women being freed from death rows across America involve, more often than not, media exposure of prosecutorial and police misconduct.

In capital cases where I was lead counsel, I have had a productive relationship with some media reporters who showed integrity and demonstrated that their editors would not interfere with accurate reporting. In one case, reporters investigated claims that a client was falsely accused and publicized their findings. They helped create the atmosphere in which the client was vindicated. In another case, a reporter was able to find and interview witnesses who would not talk to defense investigators. We could then contact and subpoena those witnesses.

On the other hand, we have seen the malign influence of media coverage that takes one side of the case, uses sound-bite journalism to maintain a one-sided position and creates grave risks of unfair trial. The accusations against basketball star Kobe Bryant, later shown to have been false, gained national and international credibility in the hands of reporters

who accepted the prosecution and police version of events
and ignored, misstated, or derided the defense assertions.

Reporters and their editors want to serve their customers in ways that make the customers listen, look, or read.
They focus on sensational allegations and on the community's natural desire to be protected from criminals. In order to
understand how and when to deal with the media, and to
make those decisions with courage and conviction, one
should have a sense of the market forces under which
reporters and editors work. We explored these issues in moving to change venue in the case of Terry Lee Nichols, accused
of complicity in the 1995 Oklahoma City bombing. I said this
in oral argument on the venue motion:

> We looked, Your Honor, at the quantity of media cov-
> erage; the quality of media coverage; the content of that
> coverage. We looked, Your Honor, at a simple idea that
> undergirds all of our economic system, the idea of a mar-
> ket. Mr. Armstrong helped us see that the idea of the
> market has come to play a much bigger role in editorial
> decision-making than it used to do. That is, media
> moguls, editors, are much more sensitive to responding
> to the needs of their market.
>
> Now, the government says that, "Well, this is a nation-
> al and an international story." Of course it's a national
> and an international story. It was on CNN for an hour.
> They have an exhibit like that. It was on CNN for one
> hour, one time. But, by the time the dust had settled, the
> national media dealt with aspects of the story as they

happened, and the local media replicated the whole story, beginning to end, over and over and over again.

This concept is the one that Dr. Vinson [government expert] and Dr. Bronson [defense expert] agreed is called, "salience." The media editors in this single Oklahoma market, that Mr. Armstrong found in his analysis, are doing this because they think that's what grabs their audience. That the sociologists call "salience," but it is, to trivialize it, like some darn song or jingle that you get in your head, driving down the road, and I start humming and I realize that it's that toothpaste commercial that my daughter listened to, or it's some other that I can't get it out of my head because the sheer force of repetition has put it there.

The people of Oklahoma were told over and over again—this salience thing again—that they had a special relationship to these events, and they came to believe it. But it wasn't simply that the media told them; their leaders told them; they were told by their leaders to identify themselves in this way, by Governor Keating, by Senator Inhofe. They showed that they had this sense of identity by their purchase of the memorabilia; by their adoption, their embracing of slogans, that showed the entire state and the ribbon around the Heartland. They embraced that concept as a mechanism for their recovery.

Now, there's a second part of this media difference. It isn't just that there's more in Oklahoma City. It's what Dr. Bronson called, "thematic thinking." Why is it that a prospective mock-trial jury trying the Oswald case, with

Chapter Two

all the information that it had to bring to that task, would be influenced by seeing the motion picture "JFK"? The inference is that it's because that motion picture—and I think Dr. Vinson and Dr. Bronson agree about this—has a powerful theory of events, cogently argued, with what seems to the onlooker to be evidence that it is so.

After all, we teach—when we teach young lawyers to be trial lawyers—at least I do when I've taught lawyers—we teach them that deciders perceive whole stories. Dr. Vinson tells us that when prospective jurors come to the task of deciding and bring a set of attitudes and beliefs, that they have a whole story; that trying to present evidence that's contrary to the story they've got worked out induces cognitive dissonance and causes them to engage in coping behaviors that include nonrational ignoring of the evidence, trying to rationalize it, forgetting it, minimalizing it, and so on.

We're not saying that the local media set out to prejudice anyone; we are saying that it responded to this need. Thus, the contrast between not only the quantity but the nature of the local coverage and the national coverage is what counts.

Now, there's something that's more telling, I think, than all of this, and that's what the Supreme Court has said over and over, that death is different. Well, of course it is. That's a trivial statement. But the Court, ever since *Furman v. Georgia*, has told us that death is different, and in a quite decisive way.

Why is death different? What's the procedural meaning of that? The Federal Death Penalty Act of 1994 is a weighing statute, and it places upon the jury the responsibility for assessing punishment. The jury doesn't simply find factors; it makes an ultimate decision. That's the characteristic of this statute.

A lot of studies have been done, whether *Furman v. Georgia* has achieved its purpose. There's a recent article in the *Harvard Law Review*. Well, we're not here to debate that. What is clear is that sentencer discretion in jury sentencing cases, under weighing statutes, puts before the jury a huge quantity of highly emotionally charged evidence and expressly invites the jury to do something that is unique to death cases, and, that is, to make a reasoned moral response, this free-floating decision, in which their sense of anguish, and anger, and sympathy, and so on, can expressly be considered.

Now, Your Honor stopped me yesterday because I had gone too far with Dr. Holden. I'm not sure just where I crossed the line but I hope that it was sometime after I asked him about the Bosnian Serbs, because Dr. Holden does know, as an expert, about how people identify with events: the them-versus-us. The them-versus-us here is Oklahoma versus these defendants.

Governor Keating has been quoted over and over again, repeating his mantra, "We will give these people a fair trial. Oklahomans are independent. We want to make sure we've got the right people, but, if we do, they should be executed," as though the *Furman v. Georgia* gene had dropped out of his legal chromosome makeup.

C. S. Lewis writes, in one of his letters, in that wonderful collection, that, "There are times, as for example on a dark mountain road at night, when we would give far more for a glimpse of the few feet ahead than for a vision of some far horizon." The few feet ahead that we can see tell us that in this time and place, that a jury, in this city, charged with that decision, would be one as to which one can confidently say there is this reasonable likelihood of prejudice.

Two roads, two roads, diverge before us, gathered as we are, with the decades of constitutional liberty piled so high, the anguish of the victims close at hand. To one of those roads we are beckoned, from sadness, to anger, to vengeance. Governor Keating beckons us along that road by what I suggest is deliberate design. The media have beckoned us along that road, simply by their desire to serve their market. The other road, I suggest to the Court, is the one the framers laid out for us while the memory of unfair trials in distant forums was fresh in their minds.

We neither dishonor nor deny the grief and anger of the victims, nor even their cry for vengeance. Your Honor, this is my thirtieth year in the law, and I believe, more than ever, that when we summon someone, anyone, Terry Nichols, into court, to find out whether he's going to live or die, that it is our job to construct, where we best can, a kind of sanctuary in the jungle.

I noted above that lawyers who take on controversial cases often incur not only public scorn but may also find that their colleagues do not support them. I believe that the kind of cases we take, and the way we do them, must reflect a moral and ethical sense of our role as lawyers. One need not make a public defense of a decision to do a particular case, because forcing lawyers to engage in that sort of self-justification erodes the bar's independence by undermining the idea that a lawyer decision to represent an unpopular client is entitled to deference. Partners in our law firm, or colleagues at the bar, or members of the media or public may criticize a decision to take on a particular case or client. We exercise courage when we resist pressures of that kind. I do not believe that every client is entitled to my legal services. Some clients have agendas that I cannot support or want to take positions with which I don't feel comfortable. It would be a disservice to the client and to me to take on such a case. When one is court-appointed, however, it is a different matter. Believing in the bar's duty to provide representation means accepting court appointments.

When we think of advocate's duties, Lord Brougham's statement comes to mind. In the trial of Queen Caroline, mentioned above, he was the Queen's principal advocate. The Prince of Wales—the future King George IV—had married the German princess Caroline in 1795 under pressure from his father George III. The couple loathed one another. When George III died in 1820, the about-to-be-king introduced a bill in the House of Lords to deprive Caroline of her title on the grounds that she had committed adultery. The proceedings on the bill were a trial before the entire House of Lords. Brougham was warned and even reproached for his daring tactics in defense, it being noted that he might cast such obloquy upon the king as to endanger the monarchy itself. His reply to such thoughts stressed his independence of judgment and his sense of the advocate's duty:

> I begin by assuring your lordships that the cause of the Queen as it appears in evidence does not require recrimination *at present* against the heir apparent to the crown. The evidence against her majesty does not, I feel, *now* call upon me to utter one whisper against the conduct of her illustrious consort. And I solemnly assure your lordships that but for that conviction, my lips would not at this time be closed. In this discretionary exercise of my duty, I postpone the case which I possess. Your lordships must know that I am waiving a right which belongs to me and abstaining from the use of materials that are unquestionably my own.
>
> If however I should hereafter think it advisable to exercise this right, let it not be vainly supposed that I or even the youngest member in the profession would hesitate to resort to such a course and fearlessly perform his duty. …
>
> I once again remind your lordships, though there are some who do not need reminding, that an advocate in the discharge of his duty knows but one person in all the world, and that person is his client. To save that client by all means, and at all hazards and costs to all others, and among all others to himself, is his first and only duty. And in performing this duty he must not regard the

alarm, the torments, the destruction which he may bring upon others. Nay, separating the duty of patriot from that of an advocate, he must go on, reckless of consequences, though it should be his unhappy fate to involve his country in confusion.

One can easily call to mind instances of media frenzy that contributed to injustice, and lawyers who fed the fire of sensational coverage. The media is shielded by the First Amendment from punishment and prior restraint, subject to the clear and present danger standard. Lawyers may, and sometimes should, deal with the media subject to the ethical rules that prohibit conduct that will have a substantial likelihood of adverse effect on a judicial proceeding. These rules, however, do not define when the lawyer must exercise the right kind of courage in media dealings.

Some lawyers, burned by the way media sound-bite journalists have treated them and their clients, refuse to deal with the press at all. They are like the cat that Mark Twain described:

> We should be careful to get out of an experience only the wisdom that is in it—and stop there; lest we be like the cat that sits down on a hot stove lid. She will never sit on a hot stove lid again—and that is well; but also she will never sit down on a cold one anymore.

It takes courage to refuse media blandishments to get fifteen minutes of fame as the lawyer in a high-profile case. In the Terry Nichols case, my co-counsel Ron Woods and I would not hold street-corner interviews with the pack of TV and print media reporters. We would say something like, "Judge Matsch likes to be the first one to hear our arguments, and we intend to honor that." Or, "We have a lot of confidence in these jurors. We want them to hear the evidence in the courtroom, not as it may filter through from the media." We would and did appear in formats and settings where our words would not be chopped up, and there we focused on the legal and social issues raised by the case. We did this in the interest of our client.

Beyond the client's interest is the plain truth that criminal defense lawyers are much more likely to be hauled up on ethics charges for media contact than are prosecutors and their allies. And when a case involves a significant social issue as well as a client's individual well-being, media contact may require courage because it courts disfavor with the bar.

Consider the story of a courageous lawyer named Dominic Gentile. Gentile is a well-respected trial lawyer in Las Vegas, Nev. His client was Grady Sanders, who owned a storage company where customers could rent locked vaults. The Las Vegas Metropolitan Police rented vault space and stored money and narcotics to use in sting operations. The police did not tell Sanders what was in the vault. Money and drugs went missing. For months, the police denied responsibility for the thefts, and blamed Sanders. Eventually, on Feb. 5, 1988, Sanders was indicted. The night before arraignment, Gentile studied the applicable ethics rules and discussed the media coverage issues with other lawyers. Gentile advised Sanders not to talk to the media. Gentile refused to speak to reporters at the courthouse when Sanders was arraigned.

After arraignment, Gentile held a televised press conference. He said that his client was innocent, and that the trial evidence would show that "crooked" police officers had stolen the money and drugs. He held no other press conferences after this. At trial, in August 1988, no juror reported on voir dire remembering Gentile's press conference. Gentile presented evidence, during the defense case, in support of his theory that the police had taken the drugs and money. The jury acquitted Sanders. One week later, the Nevada Bar began disciplinary proceedings against Gentile.

Gentile might have accepted the bar's reprimand, but did not. He showed the courage to challenge it, in the Nevada Supreme Court, and the U.S. Supreme Court. He won 5 to 4. The Court held that the ethics rule on press comment was unconstitutionally void for vagueness in violation of the First Amendment. Most jurisdictions have adopted a revised version of ABA Model Rule 3.6, and then added a special rule, 3.8, governing prosecutor speech. This additional rule recognizes that pretrial publicity generated from government sources often has an early and irremediable prejudicial effect. Counsel in high-profile cases have a dual role—as advocates for a client and as public citizens with as much a duty as a right to comment on the issues raised by their cases. This has been part of our legal tradition for decades. Rules 3.6 and 3.8 recognize that counsel has a right to be heard, consistent with the obligation not to create or foster a substantial likelihood of prejudice to a fair proceeding.

I have been involved in some high-profile cases, and I wrote these words based on my experience:

> We recognize ... that prosecutors have heightened obligations to their adversaries, the court and the community. They have a heightened responsibility to seek a fair and just result. Why is this so? It could be a special instance of a general rule. The state has a great deal more power to inflict harm that any private individual or group of individuals and the state is inherently, inevitably a recidivist, a repeat offender. Out of this realization comes the Supreme Court's remarks in decision in *Berger v. United States* and the Sixth Circuit's eloquent discussion in the *Demjanjuk* case. More recently, we have seen the case of Durham County District Attorney Mike Nifong and the Duke lacrosse matter. Nifong was disbarred for lack of candor and for media comments that created a serious risk to trial fairness.

I can remember a few years ago being asked by the AFL-CIO to go down and help represent the Charleston Five, dock workers charged with using their heads to make offensive contact with police batons in a demonstration that they had a permit to have down on the Charleston docks against a non-union operator. When the longshoremen showed up down by the docks, they confronted six hundred riot police who were ready to break up their march and beat up them up. The local sheriff refused to prosecute the longshoremen, except perhaps for a misdemeanor or two. South Carolina's

Attorney General Charlie Condon then announced that South Carolina needed to make an example out of these "violent" union members. The reason for the riot police and their tactics became clear. This was a plan at the highest level of state government to attack the union's power and influence in the busy Charleston port. Condon convened a special grand jury and headed a team of special prosecutors. Five dockworkers were indicted for felony riot, which is a vague and broad common law offense in South Carolina.

When I first got into the case, I read the Attorney General's press conferences. I then wrote a motion to disqualify him from proceeding further in the case on the grounds that he had already violated ethical rules by making media statements that he knew or should have known had a substantial likelihood of prejudicing a judicial proceeding. I relied of course on the rules of professional responsibility that had been rewritten in the wake of *Gentile v. State Bar of Nevada.*

Having filed that motion and others directed at First Amendment and criminal procedure issues in the case, I went to Charleston for a pretrial hearing. The Charleston lawyers working on the case and I went to the state court building on the outskirts of Charleston. The presiding judge, called us into his chambers and showed us that morning's edition of the local paper. The Attorney General had held a press conference the evening before, announcing he was withdrawing from the case.

That was a good event for us because the judge,

regardless of what he felt about it before, made clear that to withdraw an appearance in his court you generally filed a motion to withdraw, rather than holding a press conference. However, construing the press statement as a motion, it was granted and the Attorney General would no longer be welcome to practice there.

In the State prosecution of Terry Nichols, the trial court disqualified Oklahoma County District Attorney William Macy from the case based on his prejudicially inflammatory media statements.

Knowing the rules about what a lawyer may permissibly do is less than half the way to understanding what the lawyer should do. The great trial lawyer Hal Haddon says that choosing to deal with the media is like grabbing a wolf by the ears. He is right, in that the reporters are looking for a story, not necessarily for a fair and impartial retelling of events. Exercise restraint. If you express yourself to the media, do so in sound-bite form. If you can establish a relationship with a reporter, and be assured of more thoughtful coverage, you may decide to have a longer and deeper relationship with that reporter. But the story of the case is not about you—it is about the client, and your fifteen minutes of fame can get in the way of the client's best interest.

Notes

- The cited essays are Michael E. Tigar, "The Most Impertinent Question," *Litigation*, Spring 2003, and "The Power of Myth: Justice, Signs & Symbols in Criminal Trials," *Litigation*, Fall 1999, p. 25, available online at WESTLAW.

- *United States v. Reynolds*, 345 U.S. 1 (1953).

- *United States v. Coplon*, 185 F.2d 629, 638 (2d Cir. 1950).

- The discussion of Grotius owes much to Benjamin Straumann, " 'Ancient Caesarian Lawyers' in a State of Nature: Roman Tradition and Natural Rights in Hugo Grotius's *De iure praedae*," 34 *Political Theory* 328 (2006).

- The Yevtushenko poem is entitled "Talk."

- The *Texas Law Review* article is "Defending: an essay." 74 *Tex. L. Rev.* 101 (1995).

- On seditious libel, see my essay, "Crime-Talk, Rights-Talk and Doubletalk," 65 *Tex. L. Rev.* 101 (1986).

- Professor Barbara Bergman has written about the Sweet case in *Trial Stories*.

- The information about lawyer behavior and lack of preparation relies on David M. Trubek, et al., "The Costs of Ordinary Litigation," 31 *U.C.L.A. L. Rev.* 72 (1983).

- The 2001 essay is, "Lawyers, Jails and the Law's Fake Bargains," *Monthly Review*, July/August 2001.

- *Cooper v. Superior Court*, 55 Cal. 2d 291, 359 P.2d 274 (1961).

- The contempt case is *In re Dellinger*, 502 F.2d 813 (7th Cir. 1974).

- The 1988 article is, "Jury Argument: You, the Facts, and the Law," 14 *Litigation* 19, Summer 1988.

- *Gentile v. State Bar of Nevada*, 501 U.S. 1030 (1991). On WESTLAW, you can read our Supreme Court briefs, which trace the history of lawyer speech on matters of public concern.

- The Wikipedia entry on Mike Nifong is generally accurate, and contains citations to other sources: http://en.wikipedia.org/wiki/Mike_Nifong.

- Suzan Erem & E. Paul Durrenberger, "On the Global Waterfront: The Fight to Free the Charleston 5" (2007) tells the Charleston story in context. It is a superb study of lawyers working in the media spotlight, and of representing an organization under attack. My quoted comments were part of a lecture that morphed into an article, "What Lawyers, What Edge?" 36 *Hofstra L. Rev.* 521 (2007).

Rapport

Rapport with Your Client

I sat at dinner in a small northern Indiana town, with a group of public defenders. All of them had grown up with a few miles of where we were. Most of their fathers and mothers were first- or second-generation Americans, drawn to this area by the steel mills and related occupations. Their ancestry was Irish, Ukrainian, Italian, and Serbian. They had gone away to law schools no more than 150 miles from their home towns. They spoke of their clients and cases as one would speak of a neighbor or acquaintance. They were lucky.

Most of us are not so lucky. Our clients are different from us. Their social backgrounds, their concerns, and the manner of expressing them are unfamiliar to us. For us, rapport with our clients is something we must learn to do. I mean "must learn," as in needs to be done. Rapport is not optional if we are to succeed.

As it turned out, the public defender seated next to me at dinner had recently tried his first capital case. I found this out only later in the evening talking to one of his colleagues. The client, an African-American, had committed several brutal homicides. The client and the crime were so far outside this lawyer's previous life experience that he had to learn an entirely new set of skills to do the case. The lawyer's family traced its origins to Eastern Europe, and he grew up in a white community surrounded by values brought from that place.

In part, the newness of the experience was due to the case being capital. The ABA Guidelines for capital defense counsel tell the lawyer to consult with the client within twenty-four hours of being appointed. Given that the defendant's case in mitigation will involve a personal and family history, the Guidelines say that the defense team must go back three generations in investigating the defendant's background. Environmental and hereditary factors may lurk back there, and evidence of them provide guidance about the defendant. In capital cases, the Supreme Court has emphasized that no matter how egregious the crime, the defendant's personal characteristics may be shown in mitigation.

This lawyer came slowly to see that he needed new tools and a new outlook on understanding the case and the client. He took on the task, built a defense team, and developed the necessary rapport and understanding. He obtained a life verdict.

The story of this lawyer is relevant to everyone's trial practice. Inevitably, our clients will have different life experiences than our own. They present us with problems that we have not ourselves experienced. But there is more. Building rapport with his client transformed this lawyer. He learned that his client's aspirations and human condition were not so different from his own after all.

A client is not a set of problems to solve, but a complex human being who happens to have problems. The client comes to you to help understand how the structures of legal rules can help solve the problem. This client may at some point testify in deposition or at trial, and will face decisions about settling the case. You must draw out from the client details that may be embarrassing or that he or she conceals from others in daily life. Unless you have developed rapport, you cannot understand how well the client will do under examination or facing the stress of litigation, or how vulnerable his or her story may be to attack.

There is this same need for rapport even if your client is not a human but an organization. Indeed, the problem of having rapport may even be more complicated and difficult. Corporate and other organizational leaders are often impatient with litigation and unwilling to spend the necessary time with counsel. Then, when it comes time to choose the corporate representative who will be deposed or attend the trial, the unprepared or arrogant corporate spokesperson moves the jurors to impatience and anger.

With the organizational client, rapport begins by identifying the person or people who will speak for the group. Insist that this person be available to help make contact with people in the organization you will need to consult, and to explain the costs and strategies of litigation to organizational decision-makers. You must convince this person that institutional prejudices and loyalties can sometimes interfere with sound litigation strategy, and enlist his or her aid in making that point inside the institution.

In one major litigation project at a major corporation, key employees were reluctant to take time from their duties to help the litigation teams because they feared that their performance reports would suffer. The corporate general counsel's office convinced management to make litigation assistance a part of those employees' job descriptions, so that their cooperation would be considered and rewarded equally with their regular job performance. Obviously, such a system could not overstate the importance of the litigation contribution, for that might look like paying for testimony or at least having an improper influence on potential witnesses.

Sometimes, you will get the sense that the organization is divided on how to approach the litigation, and you will spend a lot of time in meetings helping to work out the differences. If you are lead counsel, you must insist on a measure of autonomy and on having a decision structure that can function efficiently and, when necessary, quickly. Early in the representation, work out a case plan with the organization's responsible leaders and get the authority to execute it. Few things are more frustrating to outside counsel, and more potentially dangerous for the client, than a team that limps along and is unable to respond to the challenges that litigation inevitably brings.

These days, many corporate and other organizational clients impose limits on how retained counsel are to work. Some of these limits are useful ways of saving costs. However, some corporations put up barriers to lawyers' providing the most effective legal services. A lawyer should not get into the case if he or she cannot do an effective job due to unreasonable constraints. Such constraints may include limits on doing a proper investigation, on time spent preparing for court appearances, or restrictions on access to the client's own data.

It is up to you to persuade the client's responsible representatives of what an effective litigation strategy will entail, and what it will cost. To fulfill this responsibility, you must accept the responsibility of handling the case effectively, on time, and within budget. In more than forty years of working on complex litigation, one of the most frequent justified complaints by corporate general counsel is that the litigation team did not exercise this kind of control.

Rapport with Your Team

If you are lead counsel, you must be a leader. You must lead by the team approach and show your qualities of leadership in client meetings, depositions, and in the courtroom. Unfailing courtesy toward your team members, respect for and concern about their abilities and tasks, and an inclusive attitude toward the team's work are indispensable. The approach that too many firms take, of dividing up tasks that younger lawyers and paralegals are to do, without meaningful connection to the entire enterprise of the case story, is wrong. That approach disserves clients and fails to provide young lawyers with the mentoring that they need in order to take their place as the next generation of leaders.

Recently, I was asked to help a client who had been involved in major litigation that had been going on for several years. His legal bills had been large. He had hired the litigation partner of a large law firm. The client complained that this partner was traveling around the country trying this or that case, and not focused on his matter. Rather, the motions practice and other tasks were handled by two partners in a different office than the litigation partner. These two partners were helped out by several associates, each of whom would work on a particular project that needed doing, such as polishing up a motion. In addition, lawyers from two other law firms had become involved in the work. One law firm had been brought in by the firm the client had initially hired, and another law firm by the client himself to keep watch on the rest of the lawyers and help out with some legal issues. The client had also approached investigators to help gather facts, because he rightly saw that the lawyers he hired were not building the factual case as well or as quickly as they should.

What is wrong with this picture? No rapport, and no structure. Rapport begins with leadership. The lead counsel the client hired had to take charge of the case and direct all the activity toward the sole and single goal of maximizing the chances of winning. The essay on "structure of your team" in Chapter Seven deals with the organizational issues. Rapport with the team means that the lead counsel must know who is working, and on what. He or she must lead and inspire every team member, and be available on a planned basis to every team member. Of course, delegation of authority is inevitable in a big case, but never at the cost of team cohesion.

It would not be right to blame the client for acting inefficiently and indeed foolishly. The client would not know, for example, that his own reaching out to hire investigators might mean the people he hired and their work would not be protected by privilege.

I learned rapport from Edward Bennett Williams. No matter how large the case, if you were on the team you had substantial responsibility—and accountability. Ed might call you at any time of the day—and sometimes the night—to share an idea or challenge something you had written in a memo or motion draft. The huge conference table in his office was a command center for arguing over litigation decisions. In the end, we respected Ed's leadership not only for the great lawyer he was, but also because he was making us feel part of a common endeavor.

Rapport with Witnesses

During the trial of Terry Nichols, in which I was appointed counsel, our investigators found a key witness in a small Arkansas town. Her family ran an insurance agency. She had told a story that we wanted the jury to hear. But when she arrived in Denver, she resented being separated from home and family. She was angry and afraid to take the stand. She wondered aloud why she should help give a defense to a man accused of multiple murders.

Jane Tigar, my wife and law partner, called on her at her hotel room. They talked for a couple of hours. Jane explained the significance of the right to a defense. She pointed out that the witness would be contradicting the testimony of a man who had confronted her in her office and behaved in a rude and insulting manner. We were not afraid of the truth. Whatever this young woman recalled, she would have a chance to recount it.

Almost all witnesses—excepting those such as police officers and investigators who testify often—are unfamiliar with the courtroom. They often have some combination of fear and resentment about being called to testify. They mistrust the lawyer who will be examining them.

Rapport is difficult because you must examine the witness by nonleading questions. After you establish rapport outside the courtroom, you must carry it into the trial. You must help the witness with an order of questions that carries the story along. You must be interested in every question and every answer, for if you are not engaged with the witness, you cannot expect the jurors to be.

Almost every witness has special qualities that can make their testimony real, but you must have developed a real rapport with the witness to know what those qualities are. The nurse can say, "I checked the blood pressure," or "I checked the blood pressure, just as I was trained to do." The second answer dignifies the witness in the jurors' eyes, and lets the witness exhibit a quality of which he or she is proud. An experienced employee, well-briefed on antitrust risks, is better able to know if anything improper happened at a meeting than someone with less experience. A bank teller may have been trained to observe the characteristics of those at his or her workstation. A court official will have been trained to notice whether certain procedures were or were not followed. A good salesperson looks people in the eye, remembers details and listens carefully. Jurors believe that people act out the characteristics of their occupations. Learn your witness's special qualities, and integrate them into the direct examination.

In addition to making your witness comfortable with the job of testifying, you must make him or her aware of the various tools you as the lawyer have: refreshing recollection, making objections, showing pictures to the jury, filling in gaps on redirect examination. You tell the witness of these tools in order to instill confidence, to help the witness to focus on one and only one task: Do your best at answering the questions.

Introduce the witness in a way that identifies and dignifies. You want to let the jury know why this witness's testimony is going to be believable and important.

"Good morning. Will you tell the jury your name?" This question reminds the witness to speak to the jurors.

"Do you live here in Austin?" Or, if not, "What city and state do you live in?" You don't need to get more than the city and state, unless the address is important to the story.

Your next question can be, "What do you do for work?" You can leave this out or defer it if it doesn't help the narrative. Notice that, borrowing from Tony Axam of Atlanta, we don't ask the ponderous, "What is your business or occupation?" We want an answer in which the witness shares her or his vocation.

Now, end the suspense, and tell the jury what you're doing. "Do you know why you're here?"

"Yes," should be the answer, and no more.

"Why?"

"Because I saw the train run into Mr. Thompson's car." Or, "Because I was the company engineer at those meetings in 1975."

Next, consider asking a question or two that sum up what the witness is going to say. "Was the railroad crossing gate shut or open when the train ran into Mr. Thompson's car?" Or, "When you were at those meetings, did you hear anybody discuss the price at which crude oil should be sold?"

These three inquiries—what work, why are you here, and what did you see—may seem simple. If you think so, go to court and listen to the stilted introductions of witnesses— in language that neither the witness nor the jurors would ever use. Then comes a labored trudge through preliminary details. By the time the lawyer has dragged the witness to the place where something important happened, the journey has already exhausted the jurors' patience.

You must have a conversation with the witness that respects the rules of evidence, and is being held for the jurors' benefit. You must visibly care about each answer, and make each question follow on from it. You cannot write out questions for such an examination, for you will miss verbal cues to speed up or slow down, to fill in a detail. This is rapport. It begins with knowing how to listen to another person tell an interesting story.

Witnesses in My Favorite Movie

The ABA asked me, and some other lawyers, each to contribute an essay about our favorite lawyer movie. The editor
was surprised at my selection. My essay will tell you why:

> We all know that we must present jurors with a
> coherent story of the case. We sit with colleagues, and
> sometimes with consultants as well, to devise and refine
> "the story." We may forget that a story is told by people,
> to other people. The story is actually built up from the
> testimony—the personal experiences—of witnesses,
> who bring us their version of what happened and their
> sense of the justice or injustice of it. These witnesses,
> with our guidance, speak to jurors, each of whom brings
> their own set of attitudes to the process.
>
> My most telling trial experiences revolve around wit-
> nesses who made an impression on jurors: Fernando
> Chavez and his father Cesar in Fernando's trial for draft
> refusal, John Connally in his own defense, a physician
> who described the pathology of methamphetamine use.
>
> Too many lawyers fail to see and take the steps from
> imaging the story to telling it simply and persuasively. To
> do this, we must learn to share vicariously the lives and
> experiences of our clients. After all, Darrow had never
> walked down the corridors of madness as had Leopold
> and Loeb, nor ever braved a white mob while trying to
> move a black family into their home, nor lived among
> union organizers in the mines, mills and forests. Yet,
> more eloquently than any of his time, he could bring

witnesses and then summon up those images for judges and jurors.

With these my prejudices in mind, I chose a film that is not about lawyers at all, and only a little bit about law. It is a film that can teach us how to listen to people's grievances and then tell their story. "Salt of the Earth" was produced in 1954. It is about a Mine, Mill & Smelter Workers strike against a zinc mining company in New Mexico. The striking local was predominantly Hispanic, and the demands included equal pay with Anglo workers, decent living conditions in the company town, and safe working conditions. The company refused to negotiate. It closed off access to the company-owned food store. It tried to bring in scab labor.

Eventually, the company got a Taft-Hartley injunction that forbade the striking miners from picketing. At that point, the miners' wives asserted themselves and took up the picket duties. Eventually the company agreed to most of the miners' demands.

However, this was McCarthy time. Union leaders were the targets of red-baiting. One of them, Clinton Jencks, was prosecuted and eventually vindicated when the principal government witness admitted to being a perjurer.

When some principled writers and directors decided to make film about the strike, they faced all manner of difficulty. They had trouble getting financing, there were efforts to disrupt the filming, and their principal actress was arrested and deported to Mexico.

"Salt of the Earth" treats themes that fifty-four years

later remain volatile: workers' rights, health care, the efforts to divide people based on their race, ethnicity or immigration status, the struggle for gender equality.

You can order the film online and even download it, as it has passed into the public domain. As you watch it, here are the lessons for trial lawyers.

First, most of the actors were nonprofessionals— union members and others, including Juan Chacón, the male lead, who was a union local president. These people are witnesses: they are miners and miners' families, telling their own stories. If a Hollywood writer and director can encourage performances like that, you as a trial lawyer can do as well. All you must do is listen and care as deeply as those who made this film, and think as creatively about how your witnesses present themselves.

Second, the film teaches us to look deeply into the human situations that our clients bring to us, to search for causes rather than litigating about effects.

Third, the film reinforces our sense that we can—as citizens and as trial lawyers—dare to talk about fundamental issues of justice and injustice, knowing that we can awaken in jurors the desire to reaffirm what is right and change what is not.

Rapport with Judges

Building rapport with judges takes place in different settings and in different ways. In a small community, lawyers and judges know each other; they develop relationships that may or may not be cordial, but at least everybody knows what to expect. In a jurisdiction where a case is assigned to a particular judge when it is filed—"assignment jurisdictions"—the lawyer will have a chance to see the judge in action as the case moves toward trial or settlement. In a "master calendar" jurisdiction, a case is filed, and then at various stages sent out to different judges. Motions may be heard by a "law and motions" department, a request for interim relief by a judge who hears nothing but such requests for a month or more, and finally, when the parties announce ready for trial, the case goes to a "trial part." In such a system, cases can get lost, and no one judge learns anything about the case and the lawyers.

I greatly prefer the assignment system, for that system makes it possible to move the case along and to acquaint the judge with the issues in an orderly way. Even in such a system, however, heavy caseloads and inattentive judges can make it impossible to build rapport. Some judges seem content to receive written briefs on issues, ponder or have their law clerks ponder the issues, and then issue written orders without ever giving the lawyers a chance to be heard.

In short, I acknowledge the difficulties that lawyers and litigants face in this time of crowded calendars. However, in order to succeed at trial, or in pretrial settlement discussions with judicial participation, or on important motions, it is vital to understand the judge's preferences and temperament.

Some of the rules should be self-evident. For example, carefully prepared pleadings invite judicial approval, sloppy ones quickly gain the lawyer a bad reputation.

However, here are some thoughts based on experience. In drafting a complaint or answer I always include a paragraph on "the nature of the case," and good descriptions of the parties in the paragraphs that set out their status. I write the complaint or answer in plain English, and edit it to avoid legalisms and repetition. If the judge or law clerk glances over the document, he or she will quickly grasp the essence of the case.

I seek oral argument on almost every motion. I invoke the rules that in almost all jurisdictions call for an early status conference to put the litigation on track. I show up ready to comply with reasonable limits on the extent and timing of discovery and urge entry of an order to that effect.

Moving to the trial context, one must remember that jurors are disposed to accept the judge's authority, and therefore to lose respect for a lawyer who seems to be obstructive or rude. To build rapport during the trial, the lawyer should seek a trial rhythm that permits making needed objections and building the case, while respecting the judge's legitimate priorities and concerns. In the trial of Terry Nichols, we did the following:

- Our motions practice with Judge Matsch, once he was assigned to the case after recusal of the Oklahoma judges, was as well-done and extensive as possible.
- Given the intense media interest, and Judge Matsch's known preference to have the case tried in the courtroom and not in the press, we sought orders governing lawyer speech, and sealing orders to keep potentially inadmissible discovery material out of the public eye.

Our success in this respect can be tracked on the Westlaw file OKLA-TRANS.

- We insisted that every critical stage of pretrial proceedings be held in public, including the jurors filling out the
jury questionnaire, and rulings on challenges for cause.
We believed that if a judge is required to make and justify rulings in public, there is more chance of his being
respectful to advocates and giving the impression of fairness. While we cannot prove we were right, we did seem
to have more challenges sustained than the McVeigh
team, and we were able to do a more thorough voir dire
than that team was accorded.

- We took the position that when jurors were in the courthouse, they should be hearing evidence, not lingering in
the jury room while lawyers wrangled. We proposed to
file short written memoranda almost every trial day raising evidentiary and legal points. We suggested hearing
disputed matters during regular court recesses or at the
beginning or end of the trial day. Given that the trial
would last for several months, we suggested that the jury
hear evidence only four days per week, to give jurors
time to attend to their normal business, and to allow
time for extended consideration of legal issues. Judge
Matsch adopted our proposed schedule because it fit his
perception of how the jurors should be accommodated,
and respected his preferences for hearing and deciding
legal and evidentiary issues. Judge Matsch knew that
onlookers were going to compare his handling of the
trial with the way Judge Ito had handled the O.J. Simp-

son murder case. In that case, jurors were constantly being excused from the courtroom for long wrangles on legal issues. Paying attention to the jurors' use of time is also an important ingredient of rapport with jurors.

In a tax-evasion case thirty years ago, my friend Morton Susman and I represented a defendant before a federal judge generally regarded as very deferential to the prosecution. We repeatedly sought access to government files we believed contained exculpatory evidence. Every trial day, we filed a short memorandum showing how the previous day's proceedings supported our demands, and citing authority. After about two weeks of this, the judge came on the bench one afternoon, granted our motion and explained that he had finally seen the point of our demands.

Rapport with Jurors

Rapport begins with jury selection. Jury selection begins, if possible, with a juror questionnaire that asks jurors their names, addresses, family situation, prior jury service, military service, community organizations, media preferences, and then detailed attitudes toward the main issues in the case. Ask around and find a questionnaire being used in your area.

When the jurors show up, you must ask the trial judge for at least some opportunity for lawyer voir dire. Let's face it, judges have entirely different motives in jury selection, and most of them are not very good at it anyway. Perhaps there should be a note in the "Courage" chapter on the need to give judges this unhappy news.

I cannot "teach" voir dire. We can only give you some ideas and approaches. To practice voir dire techniques, try having a conversation with somebody you don't know and finding out as much as you can about them with open-ended questions. Almost all jurors will tell you they will be fair. They know what "fair" means—to them.

In a case involving alleged conspiracy with terrorists, the judge did all the voir dire, based on questions submitted by the lawyers. He would ask follow-up questions only reluctantly, as he was convinced that he was finding jurors who would be "fair and impartial." The case had many hot-button issues for jurors. One prospective juror had said on the questionnaire that his son had been in the military in Iraq, but was no longer. The judge was willing to confirm that answer and leave it there. We pressed for the judge to ask whether the juror had discussed Iraq with his son. The judge finally agreed, even though it meant that the juror would have to return the next day for these additional questions.

The following morning the juror said he had talked to his son.

"Was that here in New York?

"No, he is still in Iraq. He works for one of those private firms."

"What did you talk about?" asked the judge. (Finally, a real open-ended question.)

"About all this torture stuff that is going on." (It was the time of the Abu Ghraib scandals.)

The judge was interested. He simply said, "Yes?"

"Well," the juror said, becoming more voluble, "all this stuff about torture. The way those people over there behave, of course you got to beat their butts. We just don't understand the problem."

The judge visibly recoiled from this outpouring of hateful thought. Regrettably, the episode did not change the pattern of voir dire. It did, however, reinforce the idea that open-ended questions and a decent respect for honest answers are the fundamental precepts of good voir dire.

I reiterate that jurors will be eyewitnesses and earwitnesses to trial events. They share all the good and difficult qualities of any such witness. You must think about this insight during voir dire and during every moment of the trial.

From the jury questionnaire you get subjects about which to talk with the jurors. Be interested in what the jurors want. You cannot feign this interest. You have to practice listening to people. In a particular case, you might want to do a little research at night to prepare for voir dire the next day. In one trial, we got on the Internet to find out about the different meanings of bioenergetics. We needed to talk to a juror about his interest in this subject to probe whether he was really a serious researcher with a scientific bent, or had a more superficial knowledge and interest. Our research led to questions that led us to believe he would be an excellent juror, a challenge for cause by the other side was denied, and the other side had to use a peremptory challenge.

Here is an article from the *Daily Oklahoman* about jury

selection in the Nichols case. The newspaper article is in Helvetica (bold) typeface, my comments in Century (roman):

Michael Tigar is living up to his reputation.

The lead attorney for bombing defendant Terry Nichols can be brilliant in court and he can be a show-off.

In the three weeks of jury selection, he's quoted Latin to the Latin teacher, talked landmarks in Paris with a woman who went to college there and asked fans of the novel "The Horse Whisperer" if they support that gentle approach to breaking horses. [Read on to know why we would explore things in which jurors are interested. This is not "making conversation"—it is a way to find out how these folks approach difficult issues. If you can find out what books jurors have read recently, you know that a given juror reads books, and you will find that a lot of them have read books about the legal system—Grisham or Turow. *The Horse Whisperer* was a popular book at the time of this voir dire. It said something about an approach to people and issues.]

He also kept skilled prosecutors on their toes, rattled the veteran judge and scored points with potential jurors.

The University of Texas law professor is widely regarded as one of the best criminal defense attorneys in the country, and his legal victories are legendary. And he believes in being himself in court.

"Jurors are quick to know who is being a phony and

who is not," he warned in his 1993 book to fellow trial lawyers, urging them to find "your own voice ... and not a borrowed one."

"None of us is good enough to maintain pretense through a long trial," he wrote.

Tigar was appointed in 1995 to defend Nichols, who is accused of helping convicted bomber Timothy McVeigh blow up the Alfred P. Murrah Federal Building in Oklahoma City.

"He's definitely different than Stephen Jones," one bombing victim said of Tigar, comparing him with McVeigh's former defense attorney.

"To me, he seems to be more involved," said the victim, David Sykes, who was delivering mail to the Murrah Building when the bomb exploded.

True to his Texas background, Tigar, 56, typically wears the silver Western belt buckle he says his mother gave him. He walks briskly into the courtroom in the same black cowboy boots, once joking he had a bad day when he switched to another pair.

He sits next to Nichols at the defense table—which he had scooted over to get a better view of the candidates. He often puts his large right hand on Nichols' shoulder, as if to comfort his client. [See the material below on courtroom control.]

One morning, he walked to the spectator benches to kiss Nichols' mother, Joyce Wilt, on the cheek before the judge arrived.

Jury candidates are questioned one at a time, and

U.S. District Judge Richard Matsch and prosecutors go first.

So Tigar, waiting his turn, makes listening an interactive exchange. Leaning toward the candidate with shoulders slumped, he holds a firm grin and bobs his head in response to certain answers. [Don't make a big show of this, but you are maintaining eye contact with the jurors as they answer your opponent's questions. No big gestures, but one theory of voir dire is to give positive reinforcement for good answers.]

When his time comes, he carries his imposing figure to the podium, where his baritone voice commands the room.

"My name is Michael Tigar," he tells the candidate. "And Ron Woods, sitting right there, and I are lawyers. We were appointed ... shortly after the bombing to help out Terry Nichols. And I'd like to follow up on some of the things that were asked and spend a little time with you."

Tigar's folksy manner often gets results—candidates respond more candidly.

They are engaged by his knowledge as he sprinkles in references to bioenergetics, farming, birthing methods—whatever applies. [These are not random references, but questions about the juror's interests.]

He also is a master of the oddball question.

"You milk the goat?" he asked one juror candidate, whose family raised a few animals as pets outside Denver.

"No. No," she said.

Tigar wants to know whether candidates choose spanking or time-outs with their children. [In a criminal case, this is a key question, particularly when the jury will decide punishment. I think it also illuminates juror attitudes in any case where punitive damages or a theory of deterrence are in issue. However, some jurors may think that questions about child-rearing are personal. In this death penalty case, one will have told the jurors that there will be questions about their ideas of proper punishment.]

He asked a study hall supervisor how he decides who is right when there is a classroom fight. [The study hall supervisor decides "cases" all the time, such as when there is a fight in school. How does he do it? Does he listen to both sides? Does he find it hard to set aside some preconceived idea based on who is involved?] He asked a school bus driver how students would describe her. [Tough but fair? Caring? Safe driver? How?]

From No. 52, a nursing assistant who thought death was too easy for a criminal, Tigar wanted to know what she thought a crook should contemplate while in prison.

"That they would regret what they've done and that they would know that they have committed a crime that is wrong," she replied.

He sometimes goes out of his way to not seem overbearing when he is getting unsatisfactory answers and has to ask more questions.

"Well, I hear you say, 'I think I would,' " he said softly to one candidate. "It's like if my wife said, 'Do you love me?' and I said, 'I think I do,' she'd want to ask another question." [This approach, like many others in our voir dire, was suggested by Robert Hirschhorn. If a juror doesn't answer your questions directly, you need to keep on asking. Then when you get a candid answer, you need to say, "Thank you. I know this is difficult territory."]

Tigar impressed a Teamsters member by describing the logo on his union handbook.

"You still get a little booklet there with the two pictures of the horses in front looking at each other?" Tigar asked him.

"Right," he said. [We knew from the questionnaire that this juror was a loyal union member. He had been on strike with his union. Under his contract, he is paid his full wage during jury service. He had read his contract and knew his rights in this respect. He is therefore the kind of thoughtful, intelligent juror one might want. It is important to show respect for somebody who goes to that trouble to prepare to meet you. As for knowing what is on the Teamster contract—the logo—that is old knowledge we happened to have, but if you needed to understand how union contracts provide for jury service, you should study that before you talk to this juror.]

Tigar even spoke the language of No. 763, a psychic and energy reading enthusiast who believed her karma would catch up with her if she sentenced someone to death.

"Now, much of your reading is about the energy in the human body. Is that right?" Tigar began.

"Right," she said.

"I mean, chakras are—well, how would you define a chakra?"

"I would say the chakras are points in the body, in the energy body that interact with the physical body; and they're data centers and energy centers where we're receiving and energy is leaving our bodies," she said.

"And in your view, do they occur along meridians?" Tigar asked.

"Yes."

"So that there are meridians of energy that run in the body and along these are the chakras that are centers; is that—" he said.

"That's correct."

"And is that based on a study of eastern medicine?" Tigar said.

"That's an ancient knowledge, yes," she replied. [See above. We wanted to know just how serious this juror was. The other side wanted to portray her as a flake. She wasn't.]

When No. 657 turned out to be a Latin teacher, prosecutors and reporters knew what to expect as Tigar approached the podium.

He didn't disappoint.

"Have you ever heard the expression, 'Ubi societas ibi jus' " he said, then gave the translation. " 'Wherever there is society, there is this idea of justice.' ... My pronunciation is wrong, please don't grade my paper; but there's this social structure within which we all live that defines ... what the rules are?"

"Uh-huh," No. 657 said.

Tigar sometimes slips in a point during his questioning—kind of to get potential jurors thinking ahead to his defense.

Jurors are expected to hear testimony that Nichols set off small explosives with his son in Kansas and a brother in Michigan. The defense will contend they were just having fun.

So, Tigar took special notice when a school bus driver wrote on her questionnaire that she had a friend with a homemade cannon.

"Made a big noise?" he asked.

"Yeah," she answered.

"Did everybody enjoy that?"

"Yeah," she said. "I guess so. Sometimes it was pretty loud."

"Well, you wouldn't jump to the conclusion that some fellow that wanted to set off things that made a noise on the Fourth of July was a bomber, would you?" the defense attorney said.

"No," she said.

"Wouldn't be logical?" he asked.

"No," she said again.

Point made. [Voir dire is not the place to get commitments on the facts. But you can ask generic questions along the line "just because somebody says x is true doesn't make it so."]

It doesn't always work.

Tigar tried to use a construction superintendent's work experience to turn him around from his belief that someone who intentionally kills many people deserves the death penalty.

"Did you ever have a situation where you had a worker out on a job and you looked at him and you thought, 'Gee, you know, that's probably not going to be a very good worker,' and it turns out they just really do a great job?" Tigar asked.

"Yes," the candidate answered.

"You know, the situation (where) somebody kind of doesn't look like they're too coordinated and you put them in a house and you tell them, 'Go take and float that drywall,' and you come back and, whew, they've got a lot of square feet done?"

"Uh-huh."

"So in your life, ... you have been able to withhold judgment until you've seen how it worked out?" Tigar said.

"Sure. As the old saying goes, you can't judge a book by the cover. I don't know how anybody can judge from the outside what's on the inside." [These questions are tests about open-mindedness, and designed to get insight into how this juror makes decisions.]

Still, No. 667 was adamant about imposing the death penalty.

A few jury candidates have been put off by Tigar's manner—and said so.

A Fort Collins scientist said he had seen that manipulative behavior from attorneys when he was on previous juries. He complained of how Tigar smiled and nodded as the judge spoke to candidates Sept. 17.

"It appeared to me that he was smiling and nodding not necessarily because he was in agreement with the judge but because he was signaling to the rest of us his agreement with the judge," the scientist said. [This "scientist" is the same one who was interested in Eastern medicine. When he said on his questionnaire that he had formed some impression of the lawyers, the quoted response was his explanation of that. You must treasure these bursts of candor. Most jurors at one level or another distrust the lawyers, and here is somebody who is admitting it. Your follow-up must establish that this is a thoughtful person, and then get a commitment that the facts as proven will determine the result—not lawyer posturing.]

Another candidate, No. 848, complained, "I felt very uncomfortable with the defense. I would not want to be in a dark alley, a light alley, day or night with them." [This juror will be off for cause, so don't worry. But you need to make sure that she has not spread her ideas around the other panel members. Jurors wait together to be questioned, and if there is any strong negative impression, ask if the juror has shared it with others.]

Tigar at first had no questions, but jumped to his feet as the candidate got ready to leave.

"Excuse me, your honor. May I just put one question?" he asked.

"Yes, you may," the judge said, then joked, "In self defense? Is that name-clearing?"

But Tigar was serious.

"Ma'am," he asked, "Have you shared your views—to which you are entitled—with any of the other jurors riding in the van or in any other context?"

"No, sir," she replied.

The judge turned serious, too, telling Tigar he appreciated that question "because I didn't think of it."

Victories come in small doses.

The judge is trying to find 64 acceptable potential jurors, weeding out those who could never vote for the death penalty and those who automatically would.

Then he will let prosecutors and defense attorneys make cuts, until 12 jurors and six alternates are left. Each side gets to knock off 23.

Defense attorneys try to save their cuts for the most objectionable candidates and try to force prosecutors to waste the government's strikes.

So, defense attorneys end up trying to persuade opponents of the death penalty to consider voting for the punishment. If that happens, the judge will accept the candidate and frustrated prosecutors will have to use a strike they might have saved for someone worse.

Tigar has won admirers for his skill in swaying potential jurors to be open-minded.

It happened most dramatically with No. 474, who said, "I think that's something that should be left up to God and not for me."

Prosecutors didn't ask any questions—certain the judge would remove No. 474.

But Tigar switched the business manager's opinion by first asking if she would defend herself if foreign troops invaded American soil. By the time he was finished, she agreed to consider both life and death sentences. [Juror No. 474 seemed to us to be conscientious and open-minded. When you see a juror like that, in any case and not only one involving the death penalty, you may need to take steps to save him or her from a challenge for cause. You do this in the same way you would set up a challenge you want to make, with leading questions that suggest the answer that you want.]

Tigar has not been reluctant to take on Matsch, despite the judge's reputation for keeping tight control of his courtroom and having little patience with presumptuous attorneys.

He asked the judge to stop telling potential jurors it was OK to change in court any answers they had given under oath on written questionnaires Sept. 17. Jurors might get the impression it is permissible for government witnesses to give testimony that conflicts with previous statements, Tigar complained.

The judge agreed to change his remarks.

Tigar also complained about the "tone and content" of the judge's questioning of a computer software consultant, who thought computers might be better jurors than humans.

[After a recess, the judge apologized.]

You can practice voir dire. Sit across from somebody and ask them a series of questions about themselves. Listen to the answers. Build a mental picture of that person. This sounds easy, but is not. Too often, I see lawyers taking in juror answers in order to build their good juror/bad juror grid. They leap to a conclusion too early, like a physician who sees ten patients an hour and rattles off diagnoses. Don't be like that.

Remember that all jurors come to court with prejudices. We all have them. We dignify them by calling them intuition or common sense. So be clear with the jurors.

"We all have some prejudices. I know I do. It is our God-given right to have prejudices. Maybe you are prejudiced against lawyers who look and talk and act like I do. Or maybe you think that cases like this don't belong in court. Whatever. The point of all these questions is that maybe you have some ideas that you brought to court that mean you should sit on some other case and not on this one."

Some questions about jurors' attitudes and beliefs will seem intrusive, to them and perhaps to the judge as well. Asking a question that the juror resents can get matters off to a bad start, if that juror winds up on the panel. Ask the judge to instruct jurors that he or she understands that some may be reluctant to discuss some of the issues that will come up in voir dire, but that the judge and the parties expect and respect candid answers. Ask the judge to tell jurors that if a question raises an issue that a juror would rather discuss at the bench, the juror should say so and the court will accommodate the request.

If the court permits you to introduce yourself, do so with an explanation of why these questions are important. "You filled out the questionnaire, and then we ask you all these other personal questions. Hardly seems fair. So let me tell you some of the same things about me. My name is … I live here in … with my husband and two children …" And so on.

"Please remember," you might say, "we want your honest answers. Don't be afraid that you will offend somebody. We have heard it all." And if you are doing voir dire with a group of jurors, and get an answer that rubs the wrong way, thank the juror for candor. Follow up. If the answer reveals a disqualifying prejudice, switch to leading questions:

"I hear you saying that your opinion about insurance companies might make you lean toward somebody who is suing an insurance company, is that right?"

You should also consider following up by asking if other jurors have a different opinion than the juror who expresses something that is a negative for your side.

Notes

- The article is, "What Lawyers, What Edge?"—*Hofstra L. Rev.*—(2008)
- *Demjanjuk v. Petrovsky*, 10 F.3d 338 (6th Cir. 1994)
- *Berger v. United States*, 295 U.S. 78 (1935)

Skepticism

Cynics and Skeptics

There is a difference between skepticism and cynicism. The skeptic doubts the truth of things in order to verify. The cynic mocks the truth of things in ways that undermine all confidence that the right can be discerned.

The skeptic says, "show me," "prove it," or, when confronted with palpable nonsense, "don't pee on my boots and tell me it's a rainstorm."

Skepticism and Trust with Your Client

A client comes to us with a story. Some of it will be misremembered, perhaps an honest mistake based on reviewing inaccurate records. Some of it will be shaded, based on the client's natural inclination to gain favor with us, to make the cause appear worthy, and to reflect the natural human tendency to regard one's own actions favorably. Some of it may be outright falsehood, designed to induce us to join in an effort to gain an unfair advantage. If we are appointed counsel, there is the added difficulty: Why should this client, now held by the state and feeling

aggrieved, alienated, and mistrustful, trust us to deal honest-
ly and energetically with his situation? The well-known story
of the system that calls itself criminal justice is that there is
hardly an excess of zeal on the part of appointed counsel,
who all too often are simply additional agents in a process
that incarcerates the largest percentage of a population of
any advanced country.

But if we all recognize that human memory is fallible for
many reasons—innocent and otherwise—we will see that a
client's story must never be taken without skepticism. If we
have internalized the sacred obligation of a lawyer to give the
very best counsel and advocacy of which he or she is capa-
ble, we will see that our skepticism must be governed by the
desire to serve that obligation. When our approach to our
clients has moved from skepticism to cynicism, it is time for
a sabbatical.

When we cross-examine, we recognize—or should—that
mistakes may be of meaning, perception, memory, or veracity. And even mistakes of veracity can as easily arise from an
understandable motivation as from a conscious desire to
mislead.

The lawyer's role is delicate. Sit with the client. Listen
carefully. Ask questions. At times, redirect the interview. For
example, don't focus on the most difficult details in the first
meeting. Get a general idea of the case, then have a second
meeting where you ask questions and get answers rather
than a narrative that the client may later decide was incorrect. The balance between rapport and skepticism must be
struck with the lawyer's personal participation. One cannot

delegate it to others in the office, even though they may be present during the interviews in order to be effective as part of the litigation team.

Express skepticism by talking about the need to interview other witnesses, to gather relevant documents, to revisit and rethink as one constructs the story of the past event that is to be tried. Let the client know that if the eventual jury believes a client has been false, they will punish him or her with their verdict—not to mention the consequences that await the lawyer who defrauds the tribunal or the adversary.

Skepticism and the Human Condition

Dr. Bernard Diamond, a pioneer of forensic psychiatry, wrote an influential article entitled "The Fallacy of the Impartial Expert." His thesis was that by the time an expert has gathered data and come to a conclusion, he or she inevitably becomes a partisan of the "truth" thus discovered. So it is with almost everyone, expert or not.

John Milton wrote that "a man may be a heretic in the truth," if he believes things only because his pastor says so, or the assembly so determines. A person's interpretation of the world around and its events is shaped by biases long held and so ingrained as not to be noticeable.

A witness you intend to call is subject to all of the pressures and temptations of any other person. You must exercise skepticism in the same way you do with a client, to help that person shed prejudices, acknowledge gaps and shortcomings, and prepare to be a credible witness who does not claim too much for her recollection and insights. You must shape a direct examination that takes account of gaps in recollection, or even unfavorable details. You want the jury to hear from you and your witnesses any information that might be used to cast doubt on the witness's testimony.

> **Q:** Have you always said that the cars were 100 feet from the intersection?
>
> **A:** No, initially, I thought they were a lot closer. But then when I knew I had to come here and take the oath, I went back to the intersection and paced it off from where I had been standing to the place where the two cars crashed.

A witness may have thought about the case and become committed to a story. That story is his or her "truth." We seek information about the times the witness has been interviewed and the influences to which he has been subjected. If the influences are too great, as when there is an unduly suggestive photo array or lineup, the testimony may be excluded.

Part of skepticism is to understand the witness's path to having and holding a "truth" that he or she now embraces. If a witness's truth is the product of intolerance or prejudice, one may never be able to undermine it. If that witness has appeared for your adversary, your greatest success may come simply by drawing out the witness's preconceptions for the jurors to see.

The second category of committed witness may be willing to alter her or his story by being shown the error in a non-confrontational way:

Q: You remember telling the jury that you saw Ms. Jones at 10:00 in the morning?

A: Yes, I do.

Q: Do you remember ever saying that it was in fact at 3:00 in the afternoon?

A: No, I don't remember that.

Q: Let me show you something that might help you.

You show the witness a calendar page, or a deposition, or something with the 3:00 version. You proceed in this way because this witness is not your enemy and you wish to urge her on to the path that you consider right.

Some witnesses have become committed to their truth and will not budge with such gentle nudging. For them, you must document the process by which they arrived at their present story, and take them through that process. For example, if a witness once was unsure of an eyewitness identification, and is now rock-solid positive, there were no doubt many intermediate steps at which the police and their allies influenced her recollection. One step at a time, retrace that path, so that in summation you can talk about how memory can be shaped by conscious, and less than honorable, effort.

In the Nichols case, key government witness Michael Fortier had been interviewed by the FBI at least two dozen times, a process chronicled in a series of FBI agent reports. Right after the Oklahoma City bombing, he had denied all relevant knowledge to law enforcement while being overheard on an FBI wiretap bragging about what knowledge he had and could sell to the media. Finally, under pressure from the FBI, he tried to make a deal—immunity for himself and his wife and he would testify against McVeigh. The FBI agents told him that they didn't really need a lot more to convict McVeigh. Could Fortier talk about somebody else, such as Terry Nichols? Over time, Fortier's professed recollection about Nichols became fuller and richer. On cross-examination, I began by having Fortier acknowledge his initial statements, and his effort to make a deal. Then, I used the FBI interview reports to track his developing story.

For this sort of exercise, you must use your techniques of witness control, and have at hand all the impeaching material to control the flow of narrative. In summation, I talked to the jurors about how Fortier's story had evolved. I concluded: "The Marine Corps builds men; the FBI builds witnesses." I based this epigram on a magnificent part of Edward Bennett Williams' summation in the case of Treasury Secretary John Connally. The principal witness against Connally was Jake Jacobsen, who had bargained for leniency in exchange for testimony. Williams said:

> You know, I think in life you can bargain for and buy almost everything. You can bargain for and buy mansions and villas and priceless works of art. You can bargain for and buy fine jewelry and all the creature comforts that you can conjure up in your mind. But thank God there are some things you can't buy and you can't bargain for. You can't buy or bargain for wisdom. You

can't buy or bargain for justice, because if you do, it's injustice. You can't buy or bargain for love, because if you do, it isn't love that you get. And you can't buy or bargain for truth, because it isn't the truth that you get, it's the truth with a cloud of suspicion over it. You can buy and you can bargain for *testimony*, and that is what the prosecution did in this case.

Skepticism about Your Adversary

Old saying: You trust your mother, but you cut the cards. In more than forty years as a lawyer, my adversaries number several hundred. I approached each of them skeptically, not cynically. However, I confirm oral agreements in writing. I listen carefully. I don't accept ambiguities; I clarify them so that we all know what we have agreed. I recognize that many lawyers are driven by their clients to play at the edge of the rules—and even beyond.

In the Oklahoma bombing case of Terry Nichols, the lead prosecutors acknowledged in private that the defense was entitled to recuse the Oklahoma judges and get a change of venue. But they had orders from the highest levels of the Justice Department to oppose our motions. So we could not relax, on the off-chance that a judge would construe our lack of zeal as a concession of weakness.

In that case, as in many others where "national security" is supposedly at stake, skepticism must take many forms. The FBI and CIA agents working the case may be economical with the truth in furnishing information to the prosecutors. In those cases, you may find wisdom in John Ruskin's dictum:

> No more dangerous snare is set by the fiends for human frailty than the belief that our own enemies are also the enemies of God.

The same excesses of zeal may be found in litigation tactics during private litigation. The journals are full of commentary about scorched-earth litigation tactics, as judges and lawyers struggle for solutions. That literature is of negligible value to you in any individual case.

In all the years of practice, I come to believe that the most useful skepticism question is, "Who is in charge on the other side?" My mentor Edward Bennett Williams would sometimes mock an opposing lawyer (not in person but in discussions at the office) by saying, "He is like a Hartford insurance lawyer with a five thousand dollar limit." When Harold Macmillan was prime minister of the United Kingdom, and Richard A. Butler his deputy, there was a vigorous Parliamentary debate in which Butler had the leading role for his side. Harold Wilson led the Labour opposition. Butler was taking hostile questions from his own and the other side. At that point, Macmillan came into the chamber. "Stop ragging the monkey," Wilson declaimed, "here comes the organ grinder now."

Think about it. You know that more than 90 percent of your cases will be settled, and that the best path to settlement is being ready to go to trial. Many cases do not settle until the parties have assessed trial risks and benefits on the very eve of jury selection, or even as jurors are being questioned. If you are to settle, you must get the attention of whoever will decide on what will be offered or accepted. Sometimes, that is the client. With a corporate or other organizational client, such as a labor union, the decision will be made by inside counsel or a management team.

Sometimes you confront a litigation team that in fact has little if any discretion, its acts and tactics being controlled by partners in their firm or their superiors in a governmental bureaucracy. You cannot believe what you are seeing and hearing if your nominal adversary is a monkey rather than the organ grinder. This is the right kind of skepticism about your adversary. It complements the skepticism that leads you to "cut the cards," clarify ambiguity, and confirm in writing.

If the opposing litigation team is just going through the motions and not moving the case forward, figure out who is really in charge. Considering bypassing your day-to-day adversaries and conferring directly with somebody in charge. Using the rules of procedure in your court, demand a status conference. Ask the judge to require that a lawyer with full authority attend. Often, a firm will send a junior lawyer to a status conference, seeking to ensure that nothing of consequence is accomplished in terms of advancing the litigation. The trial judge has the authority to insist, and some court rules require, that the lawyers have full authority to deal with any issue, including settlement and dispositive motions. If the case is close to settlement, the judge can insist that clients be present as well, or at least available.

I recall a case in the early 1990s in which the federal government was our adversary. We had won in the court of appeals. The government could not seek certiorari unless the solicitor general of the United States approved. We sought a meeting with the solicitor general to convince him to decline to file for certiorari. I have had a number of such meetings over the years under the regimes of different solicitors general. The structural independence of the SG is modulated by each SG's inclination to follow the political objectives of the administration in which he serves. In the case of which I am speaking, a deputy attorney general attended the meeting, and it quickly became clear that the solicitor general would face considerable pressure to take the case to the Supreme Court because the administration to which the deputy AG was more directly responsible ardently desired that he do so.

On another occasion, I can recall being invited to confer with a deputy solicitor general and being surprised when heads of Department of Justice sections and an assistant attorney general, as well as two representatives from a United States attorney's office, were also present. Looking at the group, I could figure out who would be consulted, and whose concurrence would be necessary, to resolve the issue we were discussing. This is just a case of "reading the other team." You get that opportunity when you see who shows up at a settlement conference, or who comes to court when the judge insists that a "lawyer with authority" be there.

Experienced Washington lawyers know how to get an audience with the deciders in federal agencies. There has been a great deal of publicity about how this access is sometimes corrupt, but it can also be sought and used responsibly to steer a case toward favorable resolution.

Some lawyers behave irrationally in terms of litigation goals because they don't know the case. These lawyers are like the ones whose lack of preparation has been documented by studies of litigation costs. Nobody who reads these words is that kind of lawyer, who wastes his or her own time, consumes court resources unfairly and does not serve clients well. On the defense side, I have talked to lawyers retained by insurance companies who are told that they should not expend resources at an early stage—hoping that the case will go away for one reason or another. In those cases, there is an ethical issue as well as a practical one. The lawyer owes the duties of zeal and skill to the client, who is the insured, and not to the company.

Of course, one must be skeptical about the assertions of the lawyer who does not know the case. That skepticism must translate into action. File responsive pleadings, start discovery, conduct some investigation. Using whatever devices are available, confront that lawyer. He must then learn the case well enough to try or settle it, or pull back and let the case go because it was meritless to begin with.

I can recall representing a major corporation sued in federal court. The case was brought on behalf of several dozen plaintiffs. It was copycat litigation based on another lawsuit that had been filed elsewhere—except that these plaintiffs lacked many of the qualities that made the other case stronger. Corporate management at first wanted to drag the case out, doing expensive discovery, hoping that this would deter plaintiffs' counsel. We convinced them that instead of that we should promptly move for summary judgment on most of the claims. By quickly exposing the heart of the dispute, we convinced plaintiffs' counsel that there was much less to the case than he first thought, and much more risk of losing it all. We settled on favorable terms.

In this case, we had first to evaluate the merits and the potential evidence. We needed rapport with the client, and the courage to speak truths that the client might find uncomfortable. We needed to justify our skepticism about the merits of the adversary's case. And then, we had to convince the client that we should drive the case to conclusion by a direct route.

Cultivating Skepticism among Jurors

In some cases, the lawyer for one side can work the jurors into a passion early in the trial and ride that sentiment all the way home. Those cases are rare, and if you think you are in one of them, consider a change of venue or better voir dire techniques.

In almost every trial, juror skepticism is your friend. It is a two-way proposition. You cannot invite the jurors to be skeptical about the other side without inviting critical examination of your own case. We teach jurors to be skeptical by applying the principle of empowerment and its next friend, transparency—as discussed in Chapter Nine.

Earlier, I included some material on voir dire. One theme

of that material is to find out how prospective jurors use evidence and insight to decide matters in their own lives and work. A schoolteacher interrupts a fight in the schoolroom. How does she decide who is right and who is not? A mechanic makes a diagnosis of what is wrong with a car. We ask questions in voir dire to find out how people approach these issues, that is, whether and how they employ skepticism in their lives and work.

One way to encourage skepticism is to set the terms of discussion: Here is an example from a defense summation:

> I want to thank you for listening to us, for taking time away from your lives and work over the past several months to listen to the evidence; and now I'm going to ask you one more favor, if I may. It may be that you, after three hours and a half or three hours and forty-five minutes of government counsel's summation, looked inside yourself and said, well, how in the world are they going to answer that? And I'm going to ask you a favor. I'm going to ask you to let me start with a clean page.
>
> You know, I—when my two older kids were younger, sometimes they'd fight and I'd go into the next room and I'd turn to John, and I'd say, "John, what happened?"
>
> And he'd tell me some version, and then I'd turn to Katie and I'd say, "What happened?" And she'd start to tell me, and I'd start to interrupt her, say, "Well, that's not what I heard." Then I realized that I wasn't really being fair to John or to Katie unless you heard each one of them out right from the beginning before I tried to unrav-

el whatever was the difficulty. So I'm asking you that favor as Ron Woods and I try to talk about the evidence that's been received here.

Telling the Judge to Be Skeptical

Jury research tells us of cases in which jurors decide differently from the way the judge would have. In civil cases, we see these differences when judges grant discretionary motions for new trial, or even judgments notwithstanding the verdict. In criminal cases, of course, a jury verdict of acquittal places matters beyond judicial control, so we have to read books about jury behavior to see how judges think.

I remember taking over defense of a libel case several decades ago. The partner who had the case before I got it had filed, and lost, a motion to dismiss the complaint for failure to state a claim. Personally, I think that such motions are rarely meritorious in a world where notice pleading is the rule. The district judge, the late John H. Wood, had not thought much of the motion and at oral argument had roughed up the partner pretty badly.

I looked at the case and after some discovery decided that a motion for summary judgment was a good idea. The news story under attack was a fine piece of investigative journalism and, although it made some strong accusations, the reporter had good sources and we were sure that there was nothing that would raise the red flags of intentional or reckless falsehood. On the day set for oral argument of the summary judgment motion, Judge Wood was in a particularly bad mood, having been mishandled by Braniff Airlines in getting back to San Antonio from El Paso the night before.

As our case was called he said, "This motion looks an awful lot like that one filed by that other fellow that I denied. I am inclined just to give you the same ruling."

I borrowed a line from Edward Bennett Williams, "Well, Your Honor, I feel about this motion like the mountain man said about his pancakes, 'no matter how thin I make 'em, there's always two sides.'" Judge Wood laughed, and said, "You mean it is like the old boy who goes to the baseball game and asks a kid the score. The kid says, "They are ahead fifty to nothing." And the old boy says, "Aren't you discouraged?" "Heck no," says the kid, "we ain't had our ups yet."

Judges differ a great deal in their expressed willingness to be persuaded by advocacy. Some judges tell you that 95 percent of the cases are destined to come out one way, that they are professional deciders and that the advocates' oral presentations do not often make a difference. Other judges, such as Myron Bright and the late Richard Sheppard Arnold, profess to be much more open-minded and say that they change their minds often based on advocate presentations. Given that many federal and some state trial judges prefer written briefs, to be followed without oral argument by a written order, it is a real challenge to encourage a court to be skeptical enough to take a fresh look at a problem. Judge Patrick Higginbotham has written an article critical of trial judges for not taking the bench more regularly rather than resolving disputes with written orders.

In appellate courts, you must often tell the court why

oral argument should be granted. If you want oral argument on a trial court motion, ask for it in your motion, and give reasons.

- The facts and law on this motion are intricate, and we want to be sure we answer the court's questions based on our close familiarity with the record. Only oral argument can fulfill this need.

- We need an evidentiary hearing in this case because the proof is in the hands of witnesses who must be subpoenaed in order to get their testimony on the crucial, and disputed, facts.

Why discuss oral argument in a chapter on judicial skepticism? Appellate judges read briefs and come to a tentative conclusion. That conclusion may be reinforced by a memo from a law clerk, or by talking to other judges on the panel. Oral argument is the last clear chance to observe the judges' concerns and to respond to them directly. It is the opportunity to cultivate skepticism about a tentative conclusion a judge, or her colleague, has reached.

If a judge expresses hostility or even anger about your position, understand that you are being given something of a gift: At least you know where you stand. Thank the judge for her candor, and suggest that there is an alternative way of looking at things. "I appreciate Your Honor's sharing that view. Respectfully, there is another way to see the issue. Let me share that idea with the court."

On some issues, there is authority that there must, as a matter of due process, be an evidentiary hearing in the trial court before certain kinds of decisions can be made. Competency of a defendant in a criminal case is one such issue. The law and literature of summary judgment procedure tells us which issues may and may not be resolved without evidence subjected to the adversary process.

Some trial judges post tentative rulings on motion days. They believe that this practice helps counsel. Other judges say that the tentative ruling is a trap for the judge that leads him or her to have a closed mind. In some courts, the tentative rulings are really the work product of law clerks, with minimal review by the judge. Your job is to convince the judge that the tentative proposed solution is inefficient and ineffective and that there is a better way—yours. You "understand how one might take such a position, but that position doesn't take account of …"

One way to breed skepticism, which is to say an open mind, with your judge is always to be completely prepared on the facts and the law. Do not regard trial court oral argument as trivial. All opportunities to appear before the judge and argue are to be taken very seriously, because you are building a sense that you are in charge. This is especially so when the case is assigned to a single judge for the entire pretrial and trial phase.

I observed a court hearing in a high-profile case involving civil rights. I thought the government attorneys were ill-prepared and ineffective. Yet the judge listened to them and considered their arguments with the same care and attention given to the other side, whose lawyers were well-prepared. After the hearing, I sat with the judge in his chambers and asked how he managed to be patient when the lawyers' conduct seemed to give him reason to reproach them. He replied that if he lashed out at lawyers for one side, then that would become the media story of the hearing for that day and perhaps for the entire case. The lawyers would resent the tone and content of the judge's remarks and perhaps be even less cooperative in the process. The judge would make clear what he expected, but would do so even-handedly. He hoped that when he eventually decided the important issues in the litigation, that demonstrable patience with both sides would contribute to lawyer and client acceptance of what would surely be a controversial ruling.

I take two lessons from this encounter. First, I wish more judges were like this one. Second, often a judge will seem unduly patient with your opponent's obstructiveness, but in time your careful preparation and intelligent presentation—your rapport—can carry the day.

Some years ago, I wrote:

A courageous, wise, and gentle judge in Los Angeles, acquitting a defendant of draft evasion in 1972, apologized for himself and his colleagues by recalling Chesterton's words about the English judges: They are not cruel, they just get used to things. This judge knew that the law's customary rigor and customary inhumanity can be crueler than deliberate vengeance; the structure of law and legal penalties, as seen by the individuals caught up in the system, is so profoundly alienating.

Notes

- The Michael Fortier cross is available on Westlaw in the OKLA-TRANS database. Relevant excerpts are in the Nichols chapter of *Trial Stories*, and in Chapter Ten of *Examining Witnesses*.

- The Williams summation is reprinted with commentary in *Persuasion: The Litigator's Art*.

- The Diamond article is at 5 *Archives of Criminal Psychodynamics* 221 (1959).

- The work of Neil Vidmar and Shari Diamond on jury behavior is valuable. You can find references online.

- On oral argument, Myron Bright & Richard S. Arnold, "Oral Argument? It May Be Crucial!" 70 *ABAJ* 68 (Sept 1984).

- The case on a due process right to a hearing is *Panetti v. Quarterman*, 127 S.Ct. 2842 (2007)(due process hearing on competency).

- Patrick E. Higginbotham, "So Why Do We Call Them Trial Courts?" 55 *S.M.U. L. Rev.* 1405 (2002) (a good analysis of federal district judges' work habits).

Observation

"Well Observed"

Trial lawyers observe the world in a special way. I think their approach is, or ought to be, like that of the impressionist painters.

Claude Monet painted a picture of boats in the Le Havre harbor, as though seen through a mist. His brother asked him what to call the painting, so that it could be included in an exhibition. "Put 'impression,'" Monet is said to have replied. The brother thought this title too short, and changed it to "Impression of Rising Sun." From this title, an art critic who reviewed the exhibition coined the term "impressionist."

Traditional art critics decried the new "school," lamenting that its practitioners did not pursue lines and details. The work appeared to them undisciplined. If you go to a gallery and see impressionist work alongside that which preceded it, you will see what those critics were talking about. An impressionist scene of people by the seashore draws our attention to this or that important aspect of the scene. We can deduce from the way figures and objects are arranged a point of view about what we are seeing.

Much pre-impressionist work is obsessed with detail. Every figure is carefully drawn. We want to study the entire canvas for insights that may be drawn even from minor personages in dimly illuminated corners.

You, the trial lawyer, are an impressionist. The rules of procedure and evidence constrain you. Witnesses' recollections of past events are imperfect, as if seen through a mist, for that is the nature of human memory. You have a clear goal in mind—asking the jurors to focus on particular events and people to see through the mist and to focus on particular events, and on the justice of your client's cause.

I like the term "well observed." It denotes care in seeing, and discernment in selecting details that will turn out to be important. To have "well observed" means not to have let a single detail escape notice, even if that detail will eventually play no part in the trial. I once tried an income tax evasion case involving millions of dollars. Our side carefully studied one of the prosecution's exhibits that purported to show that our client received a lot of money on a transaction. But the document in fact did not support that theory, and we were able to make that point in cross-examining the government's summary witness. Jurors, talking to us afterwards, remembered that exhibit, by number and significance.

The impressionists were as skilled at drafting and painting as their predecessors. However, they focused on the "gestalt view" of conveying a mood. When one examines a Monet, for example, one sees that the mood is built up from details of light, shadow, placement, and personality. And in the end, Monet honors the same code as the trial lawyer: He does not force upon the viewer a conclusion about the scene, but has confidence that his portrayal sends a message in a way that the viewer will understand. The viewer—judge or juror—will more likely adopt the perceived significance because he or she has participated in figuring out what it means.

A part of "well observed" is respect for the principle that every character will not have equal importance in the tableau. This is the problem of flat characters and round characters. One might extend a similar classification to documents and objects—they too have relative levels of importance. This is what I wrote in *Persuasion: The Litigator's Art*:

> Any story is peopled with protagonists and observers. There will also be incidental characters who will have something more or less important to contribute. An incidental character may simply identify a document, or may play an important role as, for example, an expert witness.
>
> As you think of retelling the story in summation, you cannot expect the jurors to remember and care about every detail of every witness's life. Nor would you wish them to do so, for you would risk cluttering the story with unnecessary detail. Like the dramatist, you will spend time and energy making only a few characters "round," in the sense of exploring deeply their motivations, background, needs, strengths and weaknesses. These are the characters with whom you wish the jurors to identify, either to embrace and sponsor them or to

reject them. You want the jurors to recall the flat characters, but only as connected to some event, trait or object.

To illustrate, consider this case—Mary Johnson, an African-American, has long worked for Barkis Industries. She is in charge of purchasing. She is 35 years old, divorced and the mother of two children: a daughter, 7, and a son, 5. Ms. Johnson retains you to sue Barkis and her immediate superior, Thomas Copperfield, for racial discrimination in promotional and pay policies. In our first look at this situation, assume you have rejected the idea of a class action—you will try this case on the theory that Ms. Johnson was denied raises and promotions due to the racial bias of Copperfield, acquiesced in by upper-level management.

The trial will feature dozens of witnesses. You must decide how to present these witnesses—yours and the opponents'—memorably and persuasively. Ms. Johnson must be a round character. You must present all the details of her qualifications, her preparation for this job, her aspirations, and the unjust events at work. You have no choice in this regard, because the defense will also present her as a round character, though possessing different characteristics. They will wish to show her as unprepared, unqualified, ill-motivated. Unless the other side is stupid, some of the negative aspects will be supported by evidence; were this not so, the case would settle short of trial.

By the same token, Mr. Copperfield must also be a round character. The other side will present him as thoughtful, reasonable, careful. The evidence may offer you choices about how to present him. Is he the architect of these wrongful acts, harboring an active racial bias? Or is he going along with a policy—tacit or expressed—from those in the hierarchy above him, willing to advance himself at the expense of others? If you make the latter choice, and the evidence is there, you may want to introduce another "round" character: one of Copperfield's superiors, who directs events while staying in the background.

The point is that you must—early on—choose your major characters and identify their motivations. This is why I always insist that you start work on each case by thinking about your summation. Every day, or every week, pick up the file and "say your case." ...

We cannot, and would not want to, tell the complete story of every witness. ... Rather, we want to extract from these witnesses' stories just the relevant, important material, and present it memorably. So we will make these witnesses into flat characters, possessing only one or a few characteristics that matter. We will introduce these flat characters and give them titles, to help us identify and remember their functions.

Tony Axam and Robert Altman have called this process part of the "picture theory of trial advocacy." They tell us of a witness named Maria, who saw significant things. Maria was a maid. So the trial lawyer called her "Maria the maid" every time her name came up. Her profession gave her access to the events at issue, and the phrase conjured an image of her witnessing the events.

In our case, we might have "Micawber the personnel director." Or maybe, for our case, we would call him "Micawber the personnel *man*." If Copperfield's assistant supports the defense, we call her "Copperfield's assistant Ms. Smith." On our side, we might have "Ms. Johnson's friend Sara Ball," "the next-office man, Mr. Wilson," "the damages expert Dr. Overby."

Usually, you will identify and be able to name all the flat characters before trial begins. Sometimes a flat character can pick up a picturesque nickname as the case goes along—the doctor who helped out, the executive who couldn't remember, the accountant who made a mistake.

Learning to Observe from Different Perspectives

In law school, we read cases and try to identify the ways that one reported decision is different from another. We speak of "distinctions without a difference." That learning, which occupies a great deal of time in our first year of law school, may not help in preparing for trial. Reported decisions have a formal structure dictated by substantive and procedural rules. As the legal realists taught us, judges may be influenced by ideas and events that they do not acknowledge, such as sympathy for one party or a feeling that strict application of a rule will lead to injustice. Courts may trivialize important principles in order to decide a case on relatively technical grounds; for example, much litigation over the death penalty turns on rather esoteric notions about habeas corpus that judges on both sides of the debate have developed in order to reach results that fit their ideological predispositions.

As trial lawyers, we must learn to observe by seeing events through several lenses or sets of eyes: the jurors', the client's, the witnesses'. Some years ago, I represented a woman Air Force officer charged with consensual sexual relations with a civilian woman. The Uniform Code of Military Justice termed the conduct "sodomy." The military judge rejected arguments based on the selective prosecution of gay sex—arguments that eventually the Supreme Court would accept in *Lawrence v. Texas*. The defendant's alleged sexual partner testified for the prosecution, but we attacked her credibility on a number of grounds. The military "jury" could acquit if it disbelieved this witness. Of course, I was not present during deliberations that led to acquittal. However, I believe that at least some jurors were moved to acquit by thinking about the literal definition of sodomy. That definition covered all oral-genital contact, regardless of the gender or marital status of the participants. Under that definition, the male military officers sitting in judgment were all felons if they had ever kissed their wives below the belt. I think that realization—that "observation"—made them open to picking apart the evidence to find a basis to acquit.

In the Terry Nichols Oklahoma bombing case, the FBI search found nitromethane in Mr. Nichols' house. Nitromethane may have been an ingredient of the Oklahoma City bomb. The nitromethane was in a small bottle labeled "model airplane fuel." Our search of the house turned up a model airplane right next to where the bottle had been. In the same case, the government proved that marks on the floor of a storage shed were consistent with barrels having been stored there. Our investigation showed that the defendant's barrels were not the same size as those that had left rings on that floor. Both of these "finds" represent balloon-popping facts, deflating a significant adversary contention while casting the adversary as unobservant or unable to see the whole picture.

Then there is the story of the legendary Eugene Pincham of Chicago, representing a man charged with murdering his wife. The wife's body had never been found. Pincham's defense was based on the idea that perhaps the wife had run off and was still alive somewhere. In summation, he said,

> And members of the jury, how does the State know that she is not out there somewhere right this minute, walking around happy as can be, and (he turned toward the courtroom door), "Oh my God, there she is!"

After the furor calmed a bit, Pincham said, "You see, you all turned your heads to look at that door and that shows you have a reasonable doubt."

The jurors convicted Pincham's client. The foreperson came out of the jury room after the verdict and said, "Pretty good trick. But Mr. Pincham, your client didn't turn and look at that door!"

Using Others' Eyes and Ears— and Insights

Trial lawyering is a team sport, somewhat like sailing. When you sail, somebody is at the helm, but you rely on the eyes and ears of the entire crew. A captain also consults charts and guides prepared by experts. This is much like the lawyer who does the "stand up" work at a trial, and who brings into play all the accumulated insight of many people.

Because the deciders—the jurors and judge—will see the case as a whole picture, good trial preparation requires that you have a team and that all members of the team are involved in the entire job of preparing the case. Associates, investigators, law students, and paralegals should all under-stand the evolving vision of the case as a whole. They will do better at their assigned tasks with that understanding. Also, some of us (me included) have a habit of adopting a certain view of events and holding on to that view even when evi-dence mounts against it. A team that is encouraged to see the case as a whole and to share ideas can help prevent that sort of ossification. The best observation point is from high ground, from which one can survey the entire landscape of the litigation. All the team members should be up there where they can get a good view.

I get a lot of credit for saying in the Terry Nichols case, "He was building a life, not a bomb." We owe that thought to Cathy Robertson, who was working on the case as a parale-gal and mitigation specialist. One day, she stepped out of her office into the central room into which all office doors in our suite opened, and said those powerful words.

In short, you increase the value of rapport and skepticism by inviting others to have and share those values.

Ambiguity—for and against You

As you observe, never forget who will have the burden of proof. An element of proof may be enough to create a doubt in a criminal case. In a civil case, that single item of evidence may be enough to prevent a plaintiff from sustaining her burden. That same bit of evidence will not have the persuasive power to sustain the burden that must be borne by the party with the risk of non-persuasion. It is a question of point of view. Most evidence is ambiguous, in the sense that it can be interpreted in different ways. The burden of proof tells you who wins when the ambiguity points equally strongly in two directions.

In the Nichols closing, I tried to deal with ambiguous evidence and the prosecutor's burden of proof:

> So suppose you did look at all the facts and you respected the presumption of innocence and you didn't start out saying that Terry Nichols must have done it. Suppose you saw him as secretive, as insecure. Suppose you saw him on the twenty-first as a citizen scared, as you or I would be if we went to the police station, having seen Janet Reno on the television and knowing that we knew this guy Tim McVeigh and had been in business

with him and trying to remember it all and give them the leads: Go get those sheds; I don't know about a Ryder truck, but I do know about McVeigh; I can tell you details.

Suppose you looked at him as a man who loved his children and nurtured them. Suppose you looked at him even in the adversity that he confronted when [his son] Josh's mother wasn't around. Suppose you looked at him as married and having started another family. Suppose you looked at him as someone divorced and yet whose ex-wife was still saying, "Well, Josh can come and live with you." Suppose you understood that his marriage to [his current wife] Marife was rocky and difficult, a fact we did not try to hide from you. Suppose you understood that Marife had said, "No more McVeigh; I'm jealous, I can't stand it." Suppose you heard again the voice that morning on Friday when [his former wife, Josh's mother] Lana Padilla had insulted her, "She sleeps too late. What's she doing?" As though it's any of Lana Padilla's business; but as the great American novelist Kinky Friedman said, "ex-wives will stay with you through thick." You know, she said it, and Marife was insulted by it; and she said she was going to leave is how bad it was. She even remembered in these notes on the eighteenth: "Nice night, no arguments."

There is a wonderful illustration of point of view in the writings of Sir Arthur Conan Doyle, and I used that in a summation:

The evidence in this case—the judge is going to tell you about it and tell you about how to choose when it seems to point both ways. Circumstantial evidence—that is, evidence that somebody checked in a motel or made a phone call or did this, yes, even fingerprint evidence as we'll discuss—that circumstantial evidence, Sherlock Holmes once told Watson, is kind of like a stick on the ground. If you stand here and look, it seems to point there just as sure as could be; but if you walk around the other side and look, it points to exactly the opposite direction.

Seen and Unseen Elements of the World around Us

Each person's impression of what she sees and hears will vary depending on social, historical, cultural, and personal factors. We see the world around us and the people and objects in it. What we understand about those observations will vary depending on many things. Some of these things are summed up in the classic "hearsay dangers" of perception, memory, meaning, and veracity. We are limited by physical conditions that limit our ability to see. When we want to use the information we gather by seeing, we may not remember details. We may misinterpret what we see. Veracity? Our social and cultural biases skew our interpretation, not to mention the metaphorical "lying to oneself."

In an oft-reported study at Harvard Medical School, cats were raised in a room whose walls were painted with vertical stripes. Later, they had difficulty recognizing horizontal elements around them. The scientists concluded that specific neurons in the brain had particular functions in processing data, and the neural pathways that would otherwise have interpreted horizontal lines were undeveloped.

This study provides a way of thinking about our job of observing, interpreting, reporting, and acting upon data about a client's situation. We seek rapport and deploy skepticism so that we will understand and act upon a broader range of clues about the client's situation. "Observation" is no good unless we have learned what to look for, and have trained ourselves to see. As I have noted above, in representing a capital-case defendant, the ABA Guidelines tell us to go back three generations for information about how this person's life was shaped. In looking at evidence of a car accident, we will need help understanding signal lights, automobile construction, and road surface conditions.

G.K. Chesterton tells a magnificent tale about observation, and about the inadequacy of some questions to get relevant truth. Father Brown and his friends Angus and Flambeau are trying to solve a mystery. A man named Smythe has disappeared. Angus has told them the story of a man named Welkin:

> "Father," said Flambeau, after a pause, "upon my soul I believe it is more in your department than mine. No friend or foe has entered the house, but Smythe is gone, as if stolen by the fairies. If that is not supernatural, I—"

As he spoke they were all checked by an unusual sight; the big blue policeman came round the corner of the crescent, running. He came straight up to Brown.

"You're right, sir," he panted, "they've just found poor Mr. Smythe's body in the canal down below."

Angus put his hand wildly to his head. "Did he run down and drown himself?" he asked.

"He never came down, I'll swear," said the constable, "and he wasn't drowned either, for he died of a great stab over the heart."

"And yet you saw no one enter?" said Flambeau in a grave voice.

"Let us walk down the road a little," said the priest.

As they reached the other end of the crescent he observed abruptly, "Stupid of me! I forgot to ask the policeman something. I wonder if they found a light brown sack."

"Why a light brown sack?" asked Angus, astonished.

"Because if it was any other colored sack, the case must begin over again," said Father Brown; "but if it was a light brown sack, why, the case is finished." ...

"You must tell us all about it," said Flambeau with a strange heavy simplicity, like a child. ...

"Have you ever noticed this—that people never answer what you say? They answer what you mean—or what they think you mean. Suppose one lady says to another in a country house, 'Is anybody staying with you?' the lady doesn't answer 'Yes; the butler, the three footmen, the parlormaid, and so on,' though the parlor-

maid may be in the room, or the butler behind her chair.
She says 'There is nobody staying with us,' meaning
nobody of the sort you mean. But suppose a doctor
inquiring into an epidemic asks, 'Who is staying in the
house?' then the lady will remember the butler, the parlormaid, and the rest. All language is used like that; you
never get a question answered literally, even when you
get it answered truly. When those four quite honest men
said that no man had gone into the Mansions, they did
not really mean that no man had gone into them. They
meant no man whom they could suspect of being your
man. A man did go into the house, and did come out of
it, but they never noticed him."

"An invisible man?" inquired Angus, raising his red
eyebrows. "A mentally invisible man," said Father Brown.

A minute or two after he resumed in the same unas-
suming voice, like a man thinking his way. "Of course
you can't think of such a man, until you do think of him.
That's where his cleverness comes in. But I came to
think of him through two or three little things in the tale
Mr. Angus told us [about a man named Welkin who was
Smythe's rival for the affections of a young lady]. First,
there was the fact that this Welkin went for long walks.
And then there was the vast lot of stamp paper on the
window. And then, most of all, there were the two things
the young lady said—things that couldn't be true. Don't
get annoyed," he added hastily, noting a sudden movement of the Scotchman's head; "she thought they were
true. A person can't be quite alone in a street a second

before she receives a letter. She can't be quite alone in a street when she starts reading a letter just received. There must be somebody pretty near her; he must be mentally invisible."

"Why must there be somebody near her?" asked Angus.

"Because," said Father Brown, "barring carrier-pigeons, somebody must have brought her the letter."

"Do you really mean to say," asked Flambeau, with energy, "that Welkin carried his rival's letters to his lady?"

"Yes," said the priest. "Welkin carried his rival's letters to his lady. You see, he had to."

"Oh, I can't stand much more of this," exploded Flambeau. "Who is this fellow? What does he look like? What is the usual get-up of a mentally invisible man?"

"He is dressed rather handsomely in red, blue and gold," replied the priest promptly with precision, "and in this striking, and even showy, costume he entered Himalaya Mansions under eight human eyes; he killed Smythe in cold blood, and came down into the street again carrying the dead body in his arms—"

"Reverend sir," cried Angus, standing still, "are you raving mad, or am I?"

"You are not mad," said Brown, "only a little unobservant. You have not noticed such a man as this, for example."

He took three quick strides forward, and put his hand on the shoulder of an ordinary passing postman who had bustled by them unnoticed under the shade of the trees.

"Nobody ever notices postmen somehow," he said thoughtfully; "yet they have passions like other men, and even carry large bags where a small corpse can be stowed quite easily."

The postman, instead of turning naturally, had ducked and tumbled against the garden fence. He was a lean fair-bearded man of very ordinary appearance, but as he turned an alarmed face over his shoulder, all three men were fixed with an almost fiendish squint.

There is so much in this narrative. Nobody "sees" the postman because he is a part of the landscape, someone who could not be thought of as playing a sinister role in events. Father Brown also tells us a powerful truth about questioning, noting how the witness will answer depending not on what is asked but on what she thinks is being asked.

In Christopher Fry's play, "The Lady's Not for Burning," the outspoken soldier Thomas Mendip strides into the mayor's office and notices the mayor's clerk doing sums.

"They told me nobody was here," Mendip says.

"It would be me they meant," the clerk replies.

The "invisible man" can show up at the strangest times. At a panel discussion of general counsels, the participants all agreed that one of the scariest part of their jobs was the risk of surprise in a docket of litigation. Their experience, and justified fear, is valuable no matter how many cases you have, and no matter what your role.

One of the lawyers on the panel is general counsel of a large home appliance manufacturing company. A family sued the company on a claim that their refrigerator had caught fire and burned their home. The lawsuit claimed that the refrigerator had a design or manufacturing defect that had caused a short-circuit. The company investigators discovered that the plaintiff family used several extension cords in their home, and that the refrigerator had been connected to the wall outlet with a light-duty cord suitable only for use with table lamps. The inadequately sized wires in the cord must have heated up and caused the fire. So the company lawyer felt pretty good about the chances at trial, and even thought the case might be settled on favorable terms.

Then, the outside lawyer and the company hired a consultant who convened three focus groups to discuss the evidence and issues in the case while the lawyers looked on and listened from an adjacent room. The three focus groups all arrived at the same question: "Had the family ever called the company's authorized repair provider for service on the refrigerator? And if so, why had the service person not noted the use of the wrong extension cord and done something about it?"

This was a factual issue that the plaintiff's lawyer had never raised, and that was a surprise to the company as well. Indeed, there had been two service calls on that refrigerator. Now the case began to look very different. The general counsel drew from this experience the lesson "almost always use focus groups before trial."

I drew a different lesson. Many cases don't have a focus group budget, let alone a mock trial budget. I wonder why the plaintiff's lawyer had not so thoroughly investigated the case that the refrigerator repair record was in the case file. Every lawyer in that case—on both sides—had been going through the motions of getting ready for trial in the same old way, and had not been thinking deeply enough, with enough originality, looking at matters from all sides, saying the case every day. They had not observed.

I do not say that focus groups are a bad idea. If the budget permits, formal or informal rehearsals before such a group can help the trial team understand whether the proposed case narrative holds together. They can see hot-button issues that they might have overlooked. But the money spent on focus groups is wasted if the lawyers have not done their job of observing.

Helping Jurors to Observe

The jury is a collective institution. The judge's instructions remind jurors to deliberate together and share their insights. The jurors' mutual recollection controls, as does their collective verdict. The trial lawyer must know that individual jurors have different ways of remembering, and also that the deliberation process often yields results very different from those that would obtain if twelve people individually thought about the case and then voted without talking to each other.

At trial, we help jurors to observe by acknowledging the independent impression of each juror, as well as the group dynamic that the process requires. Because of differences in the way people receive and process information, presentation of the case must appeal to sight as well as hearing. Jury argument must be illustrated with exhibits. Witness questioning must be have a structure. All of these issues are dealt with in more detail in the chapter on presentation.

For the moment, let us consider the nature of group observation as compared with individual observation. In an experiment conducted at the University of Michigan, mock jurors were given media publicity about a sensational crime. Then, they listened to evidence about the crime. They were instructed not to pay any attention to the newspaper material they had read, which contained information that was not admissible at the trial. When polled one by one, most of these mock jurors relied on the inadmissible material in reaching a decision.

Then, the experiment was repeated: mock jurors were given the same media publicity and the same evidence, and told to deliberate together and try to come to a decision. In this instance, a majority of jurors followed the judge's instructions and did not consider the inadmissible material.

Our trial presentation is limited by the rules of evidence and procedure as well as by our own choices of what to offer and when to offer it. When we sum up, we are speaking to the jurors as a group. We are asking them individually to bring their insights and memories to bear, and collectively to do so within the rules as laid down by the trial judge. When we refer in summation to the judge's rulings on evidence, and to the jury instructions, we are seeking to shape the jurors' collective picture of what occurred. When we choose images, analogies, and metaphors, we want those to strike a responsive chord in all or almost all of the jurors.

Witnesses as Observers

I once wrote:

> Facts are mutable because we never see them in litigation. We see instead their remnants, traces, evidences, fossils—their shadows on the courthouse wall. The witnesses recount: They have perceived, do now remember, can express and want to tell the truth, more or less. Things—paper, hair, bones, pictures, bullets—parade by, each attached to a testifier who alone can give them meaning. At proceeding's end, the advocate will try to impose some order on all of this, and convince the trier that it makes a certain kind of picture.

A witness saw, heard, or felt—experienced—something. Your job is to convey the relevant part of that experience to the jurors. You must do this within the confines of substantive and procedural rules. You must ask the witness to use words, and, if possible, you will also use pictures, diagrams, or objects to complete the picture made by the words. The problem is that when the witness speaks, she has a mental picture of what happened. The jurors, collectively and individually, may interpret the witness's words to conjure a different image than the one the witness is trying to convey.

This is not a complicated idea. If I ask a group of people to get a mental picture based on a word I am going to speak, and then I say "pediatrician," some listeners will a male doctor and some a female. Something similar happens if the word is "truck," "motel," "president," "dog," and so on.

The witness's observations are worth little unless you break down your questions to the witness into small enough parts to convey exactly what you want the jurors to understand. Practice this by standing in front of the mirror and asking yourself to describe what you are wearing and the room you are in. Seek out ways to illustrate the witness's testimony. You can do this without interrupting the flow of examination by having a notebook of illustrative exhibits in front of the witness, pre-marked and pre-admitted. Depending on the courtroom configuration, you can show these on an overhead projector, an ELMO device, a TV monitor, or (enlarged) on an easel.

A second aspect of the witness as observer is helping the jurors to see why this witness is probably accurate. You are forbidden from improper vouching for the witness, but all witnesses have a reason to remember what they are telling us. The old "I looked at my watch at that very moment" is so time-worn as to be unbelievable even if true and unless the witness had a reason to mark down the time, as a police officer or health-care professional would habitually do.

However, witnesses do have reasons to remember. On the other hand, many witnesses have some characteristic that makes it likely they are right about what they saw. A nurse or doctor is trained to observe and remember. A clothing salesman remembers the size and shape of people who may be or are potential customers. A person who passes a given intersection every day remembers important details of it.

In sum, you must put your witness in the scene, and give

the jurors a vicarious experience of having been there. You want them to have a mental image of what the witness observed.

Notes

- *Lawrence v. Texas*, 539 U.S. 558 (2003).
- Jasper Fforde's work, particularly *Thursday Next in the Well of Lost Plots: A Novel*, is well worth reading for insights into how words convey images.

Preparation

Say Your Case

"Say your case" every day. If you have a docket of so many cases that a quick review of each of them is impossible, set up a schedule for "saying your case." What does this mean? Your initial story of the case, your proposed narrative, will grow and change over time. You will fill in the chronology of events with information about which witnesses and which exhibits can be used to tell the story. Your legal research will reveal additional avenues of potential liability or defense, or which avenues are closed to you. The story, or narrative, is a moving target. If you are the lead lawyer, you must have at hand a working summary of every case on your docket. You should be able to address a meeting of your team, your partners, or your clients and, as to every case, deliver in a few sentences or paragraphs the essential elements of the story. If your idea of a summary is to list upcoming deposition dates and motion hearings, you have the wrong idea.

As you say your case, imagine you are saying it at the next procedural hour of accountability. Perhaps you have a motion hearing next week, on anything from discovery to summary judgment. At any such hearing, you will begin with the story of your case, even if you must compress the story into a sentence or two to save time. The discovery you want is important because it will help to tell the client's story. The discovery you resist is wasteful and excessive because it diverges from any reasonable version of the story.

If you are lead counsel, saying your case helps you to focus on what your team needs to be doing. You mentor your team in this way because you help them to see the importance of story and to relate their work to effective advocacy. As a team member, your work is more effective if you see how it relates to the case as a whole.

Preparation: Organizing Evidence and Exhibits

This is an excerpt from *Persuasion: The Litigator's Art*:

> In my talks on trial preparation, I stress arrangement of trial materials as the most important organizational task of lead counsel. From such organization flows the best arrangement of your presentation to the jury.
>
> From the simplest case to the most complex, the biggest challenge is to organize information. Given the penchant to over-discover, the documents and depositions pile up faster than any one lawyer can absorb their contents.
>
> Yet, unless the jury believes that you are in complete command of the facts and the law, you and your client

suffer. That is the paradox. You cannot resolve it by delegating tasks to junior lawyers and paralegals and expecting to be "briefed" just before trial. You must take charge early and stay that way.

We do it with three basic documents that we insist be created early in the litigation and updated regularly. In a small case, we can do it ourselves with a paralegal/secretary. In a more complex case, these are the case control documents that a team of junior lawyers, paralegals and investigators work on. ...

The three documents are:

- chronology
- who's who
- exhibit list

The chronology is printed in landscape format—that is, across the 11-inch expanse of the page. It provides document control and witness control. It gives you an up-to-date overview of your case. It looks like this:

CHRONOLOGY OF [CASE NAME AND IDENTIFIER], DRAFT OF [DATE], PAGE [X] OF [Y] PAGES

ATTORNEY-CLIENT PRIVILEGED—ATTORNEY WORK PRODUCT

DATE	PLACE	EVENT	SOURCE	EVIDENCE

By using landscape format for printing, and 10-point type, you can get a lot of information in these cells. The heading should carry over from page to page. The date and place columns are self-explanatory. For each "event," you need a short description. Deciding how to break events down by date and time will depend on your evidence and on the importance of the event to your case. For example, on a key day, you might have fifty or more entries. If you are establishing a background fact, the date entry might cover several months, and the "event" be something like "James Johnson employed at XYZ Corp. as vice-president for Human Resources." The "source" tells you how you know the facts given under "event;" for example, by interview with a witness, by an identified document, or even by a newspaper report. The "source" column tells you at a glance how "good" or "solid" is your information. Near the beginning of trial preparation, the "evidence" column will mostly be blank. Your case preparation is designed to get admissible evidence of the "events" listed.

Let's use an example to see how this works: One allegation in your sexual harassment case is that company president John Jones called Mary Smith at home during the evening and made sexual advances. In the early stages of the case, the chronology for a portion of the day might look like this:

DATE	PLACE	EVENT	SOURCE	EVIDENCE
7/10/96, 5:10pm	Darrow, Ohio	MS leaves XYZ offices	MS interview; XYZ time records	XYZ time records; MS testimony
7/10/96, 5:40pm	Darrow, Ohio	MS arrives home	MS interview; interview with Joyce Wilson	MS testimony; Joyce Wilson testimony
7/10/96, 6:17pm	Darrow, Ohio Altgeld, Ohio	JJ calls MS and talks for ten minutes, tells MS that it would "help her to advance at XYZ if we could meet for drinks tonight"	MS interview; MS caller-ID printout	MS testimony; caller-ID printout

At the time this version is prepared, we have interviewed our client and her friend, Ms. Wilson. We have not yet deposed Jones. Our document requests are not yet answered. The chronology provides us a quick study of what evidence we need to prove the key facts about the call. We need documents from the phone company, Jones' calendars, and a deposition from Jones. When we get the documents, then the "source" column will contain our internal document control identifications.

As trial draws nearer, the "evidence" column will have actual exhibit numbers. Until then, it will include deposition exhibits. The rule is that anything in the evidence column is available and admissible. The fifth column forces you to get serious about what can be proved at trial—as opposed to being something that you "know" happened.

The second organizational keystone is the "who's who." In one case, my who's who ran to hundreds of pages. We really needed it, because we would look at the chronology and draw a blank on who was talking, or who the witness was.

The who's who is a list of witnesses by name. Every witness, even those whose names you got from the newspaper, is on the list, each with a short (one sentence) description of who this is.

The chronology and who's who are made on a word-processing program. They are therefore usable by people with minimal computer skills. They are searchable by word or phrase. …

Because the chronology may contain sensitive information about the case, and because the risks of inadvertent disclosure are high, we sometimes make two versions. One version has asterisks to note omitted information (such as privileged information that is not subject to discovery and will not be in evidence). A master copy containing all the information is kept in a safe place. As discovery rulings or tactical decisions expand the scope of producible or admissible material, information may move from the "complete" copy to the version in regular use. This might happen if you decided to use an advice-of-counsel defense in a case, which would open up previously privileged material to discovery production and to use in evidence at trial.

The third organizational item is an exhibit list. This will be in two forms. One is the form you are building for trial, and that will be turned over at pretrial. You want your list and your opponent's list. A second form, which may be required by the local rules but which you should in any event make for yourself, lists exhibits by witness. There may be some duplication in this version, as a sponsoring witness may authenticate the exhibit, but a fact witness may make better use of it.

For example, suppose you get a toll record that shows Jones' number calling Smith's number. A phone company employee may authenticate it. But you will publish it during Smith's testimony, as part of her story of the call—this helps your direct examination and corroborates her as she is testifying. You may publish a given exhibit several times during a trial, each time with a different witness. You would do this with a chart, a memorandum addressed to several people, or a record of an event that several people participated in.

The exhibit list is also a reality check, particularly in a document-intensive case. Making an exhibit list helps you test items of evidence. It helps you see which items are admissible, useful and efficient story-telling aids. …

Whether you adopt this system or some other, you must be able to see your case as a whole, and also be able to pull it apart and examine its constituent elements.

Preparation for the Tasks of Trial

This essay could be written in three words: Preparation, preparation, preparation. Despite my preference for brevity, I continue to receive evidence that lawyers do not heed this simple principle. So here are some further thoughts.

There are tasks—duties, if you will—that cannot be put off to another day. In our daily lives, we know this to be so. When we leave home on a car trip, we tell our children, "If you have to go to the bathroom, do it now. In fact, just go right now anyway." We expect the airline pilot to walk around the aircraft, and go through a detailed checklist, before taxiing away from the terminal and taking off. When the airplane is 35,000 feet in the air, it is too late to add fuel, go out and check the hydraulics, and so on.

The chronology that I have suggested above is not simply a repository of facts. In the early stages of a case, the "evidence" column remains blank, because we think we know things but have not yet found admissible testimony and exhibits to prove them. It may be that an important witness will be difficult to find. Important records may be in storage someplace.

Your potential expert witnesses cannot and should not prepare their initial reports without as full a factual basis as possible. How many times have you deposed the opponent's expert, dwelling on the fact that he or she gave an off-the-cuff opinion after a cursory review of a few documents provided by your adversary? That expert's eventual trial testimony comes to court with "hired gun" stamped all over it. Why? Lack of preparation.

Preparation is cost-effective. Think first of all the ways you can get information without using formal discovery processes. The work of a good investigator, freedom of information requests, and Internet searches invariably help you. Of course, you will try to put controls on the discovery process. Fed. R. Civ. P. 16(b) and 26(f) both provide for early conferences between the parties and with the trial judge about timing and use of discovery, as well as other case management details. To get the most from those conferences, initial preparation is essential. In timing discovery, think of requests for documents and interrogatories before resorting to depositions, which cost more in time and money.

I sat in on a meeting at a major law firm. The client had been indicted in an international fraud case. The lawyer who was to "try" the case was typical of a certain breed of trial partners. He was set for trial in a dozen cases in different parts of the country. His reputation was formidable. Trial preparation was in the hands of junior partners, associates, and paralegals. A month or two before trial, this partner would get ready by intense preparation. Until then, his contact with the case was fitful and occasional. There had been a focus group session to test themes with groups of people from the district where the case was to be tried. The results gave reason to hope.

What is wrong with this picture, versions of which are replicated in many law firms? A great deal, I think. First, in the two years since the indictment, the trial partner had not built rapport with the client. The client felt isolated and not listened to. A client who feels those frustrations is not able to be a constructive participant in the process of preparation. In a criminal case, he or she may reach out to other lawyers and advisers in ways that can harm the case.

More significantly, under these conditions, the trial partner cannot be as effective advocate as his training and experience permit. In the meeting I attended, I had reviewed the focus group results. I had read some of the pleadings. I had spent time with the client and with an investigator who was working on the case. The trial partner was not at the meeting. I set out some ideas to consider. Several of these ideas would require an investigator to find and interview witnesses, some of them in foreign countries. One idea was to have a witness or witnesses give an admissible overview of the investment situation that the client had confronted; finding such a person would be a difficult task. The lawyers present thought that at least some of my thoughts were relevant.

The next day the trial partner called on his cell phone from a distant city where he was involved in another trial. Yes, he said, he liked some of these ideas. We would have to sit down when he had the time and discuss them. Fine. Do you see the problem here? From the time you have an idea about where a potential witness might be, or what he might say, to the time when that witness is ready to take the stand, weeks, if not months, may go by. Trial preparation must be focused from the first day you meet the client. You, the lead lawyer, must begin to develop the case story with your team. You cannot expect to show up a month before a complex trial and find all is in order. By that time, it may be too late to find, let alone interview and prepare, the witness you need.

I hark back to the refrigerator story in Chapter Five. A trial team may have plenty of observers, but their work means nothing until the trial lawyer sifts through their observations and selects those that help him or her shape the story to be told at trial.

Preparation for Arguing to Judges

Argument is rationed, unfairly. In the courts of appeals, getting oral argument requires a persuasive statement why it is necessary. Courts of appeals set ten-, fifteen-, or twenty-minute arguments. Even the U.S. Supreme Court limits argument to thirty minutes on a side, and a party whose case is joined by the solicitor general must usually yield time to him. In the trial courts, judges seem increasingly inclined to issue written rulings without hearing from the lawyers. This system is in contrast to that in Canada or the United Kingdom, where argument and not written briefing is the mainstay of decision-making.

You must use the limited time available by being ready. When argument is before a multi-judge panel, you prepare by studying those judges' responses to the issues in your case. Before a single judge, you do research into his or her track record.

Your most valuable tool is the oral argument notebook. This notebook does not contain a text of the argument, to be read to the court. Some advocates, and even some authors on advocacy, suggest writing out one's argument. Experience and the emphatic opinions of judges counsel in the strongest

terms that one should never write out one's argument and
never read a prepared argument to the court. This rule even
forbids delivering a memorized rendition of a written argument. Such techniques throw away the most valuable benefit
of oral argument—the opportunity to be face-to-face with the
deciders, to look them in the eye, to try to fathom their true
views and concerns, and to respond to their questions.

The notebook should be a three-ring binder with tabs for
section. The facts and each point get a separate tab. Behind
each tab is a brief summary of what you will argue on that
point, with page citations to the portion of the briefs where
these points appear. These are your notes of argument, necessarily brief. When an advocate has notes that are too
detailed, the argument contains phraseology unsuitable for
oral presentation. It becomes stilted. Keep those notes short,
just enough to remind one of the issues. You will have the
briefs with you at the lectern in case you need them, but the
notebook must be your primary tool.

Be sure you include citations to key record references,
either to use in argument or in response to questions. Be sure
you know the basis of the appellate court's jurisdiction, especially in federal court. Be sure you have in your fact notes a
timeline of key events, including procedural events that may
bear upon the court's subject-matter jurisdiction. If you have
decided not to argue one or more points, put those tabs
behind the others, but make sure you have identified them so
that if a judge asks a question about them, you can turn to
that tab. Points you do not plan to argue but that may come
up in questioning may be labelled—on the tabs—"optional."

Another tab will have briefs of the key cases, usually in alphabetical order. If a case has a pithy quote that you can use, include that in the case brief. You may have a bucket file with copies of all the key cases, but you don't want to be rummaging in that to find something.

You should probably have a tab that says "questions." Behind that tab are the questions that you anticipate being asked, or that your mooting preparation has shown may be asked. With each question comes a short note about a proposed reply. The judges' questions will give you valuable hints about their thought process, and even about the way they are debating the case among themselves. If a judge asks one of the anticipated questions, that may be a clue as to how you will use the remainder of your argument time. For example, a prosecutor was arguing as appellee in an appeal claiming error in the sentencing process. The presiding judge of the panel asked, "Isn't any error here harmless, given the enormous discretion of sentencing judges?" The lawyer answered yes, but missed a valuable chance to pick up on the clue and turn directly to sentencing judge discretion. The presiding judge was giving a signal that the case might turn on this issue, and give the prosecutor an easy win.

In another case, the appellant in a gender-discrimination case was seeking reversal of a summary judgment for the employer. One judge on the panel combatively pointed to evidence in the record that supported the employer's position. The advocate parried these questions with "yes, but" and then an alternative explanation. She forgot for the moment to say, "Indeed, Judge X, there are different interpretations that one can put on this evidence. And because that is so, summary judgment cannot be sustained because it is the jury's job and not that of judges to make those choices. With respect to the point you just made, for example ..." This advocate forgot that answers to questions must fit, where at all possible, into the theory of one's case. Had she thought through the questions more thoroughly before argument, and had a note or two, she would not have been tempted in the heat of argument to get away from her main point.

It is important that the argument have a strong beginning and end. I like to have an opening—like a journalist's lead—that states the issues in terms that also reflect the advocate's basis position. For example, in *Gentile v. State Bar of Nevada*, the issue in the Supreme Court was whether a lawyer was permitted under bar rules and the First Amendment to make a public comment about a pending case. I began the argument by saying, "Mr. Chief Justice and may it please the Court, this case involves a truthful statement about a matter of public concern six months before a scheduled trial." I hoped this statement would encapsulate the special protections for truthful speech and political speech, and suggest that the public comment was unlikely to have prejudiced a judicial proceeding given the time between the comment and the trial. I also believe that one should have in mind a closing sentence or two.

The notebook permits flexibility in argument, as the court's questions may dictate a change of order and emphasis. The need to make such changes does not dictate that themes one came prepared to stress must or should be abandoned.

Quite the contrary: the careful planning for oral argument should not lightly be cast aside, any more than one would throw out an entire trial plan because one witness or exhibit did not perform as expected. The oral argument notebook helps the lawyer respond to a question and then return to themes planned in advance. The lawyer with a set speech cannot easily take up the challenge of questions, work in a theme that had been planned for later development, then return to the uncompleted thought that the question interrupted.

Example: A distinguished advocate was making an argument in the court of appeals in a celebrated case. He had written out a powerful and cogent argument, focusing principally on one main theme. Because of the advocate's reputation, the panel of judges was perhaps more than usually courteous, even deferential. Halfway through the advocate's presentation, the presiding judge interrupted to say that he hoped to hear something from the advocate on another important issue in the case. The advocate interrupted his set speech, made a short rather offhand remark about the issue on which the judge made inquiry, and continued reading his prepared argument. The judge was plainly taken aback. From the advocate's perspective, it was a significant opportunity wasted.

In another celebrated case, a government lawyer was reading out a prepared argument. A panel member interrupted with a question. The lawyer responded, "I'll be getting to that later in my argument." Here, of course, was more than a missed opportunity. The advocate had crossed over into overt rudeness and the presiding judge rebuked him.

The prepared argument is wrong for the same reason that writing out one's cross-examination of a key trial witness is wrong. One gives up one's place in the dynamic of litigation. One stops listening to the process. One stands to miss gifts in the form of spontaneous statements by the person to whom one is speaking; in a trial, that person is the witness, in an appellate argument it is the judges collectively.

Notes

• Material on oral argument preparation is from *Federal Appeals: Jurisdiction & Practice*, Chapter Ten.

Structure

Images of Structure

On our journey from the human plight that brings our client to us, and the story we will seek to tell at trial, we will encounter structures of story, of rules, and of procedures. The story must take account of all of them. In classical rhetoric, structure is dealt with under the heads of invention and arrangement. Arguments are said to have different structures, depending on whether the appeal is to emotion or logic. These categories are of limited help to trial lawyers. We must understand the constraints and freedoms of structures, most of which are important only in the context of trials rather than in the larger realm of persuasion generally.

I like the image of "structure" because it reminds us that the realistic possibility that we can win a case—the indeterminacy of result—is limited in many ways. If the case is "determined" or "destined," then we settle it rather than try it. Usually, we decide to try a case when we disagree with the other side about the range of possible outcomes. There are some, very few, cases in which the outcome is foreordained but we go to trial anyway:

sometimes we want to speak to a larger audience than the jury and judge, or the client wants or needs a day in court.

Cases influenced by political, racial, or ethnic considerations fall into this class. I believe strongly that the jury system is a fair and effective means of trial. I understand that public sentiment, racial, ethnic, or religious bias, unfair legal rules, dishonest advocacy, and overbearing judges may all distort the system and make particular trials and particular outcomes unfair. That is not a reason to reject the jury system in favor of judge trials: "I would rather face twelve prejudiced people than one prejudiced person," as an old lawyer once told me. It is a reason to struggle to keep the system honest, or in extreme cases to make it so.

The structures that limit indeterminacy are those of legal rules—substantive and procedural—and advocate skill. They are the subject of what follows.

Structure of Legal Rules

When the client tells us her story, we ask ourselves whether that story if proven could sustain a claim or defense. It is vital that we identify every plausible claim or defense within the story. We may not be able to do this at the outset, but, as we observe and investigate, we add to our initial list. Telling the story helps to create that bond between lawyer and client. "We tell stories to talk out the trouble in our lives, trouble so often unspeakable," William Kittredge wrote.

In the old common-law system, claims and defenses had to fit narrow categories, and lawyers were required to choose among theories at an early procedural hour. No more. Notice pleading is the norm. We plead facts, not legal theories, and we plead generally to take account of the way that theories may shift as time goes by. This procedural liberality must not lull us into sloppy thinking.

If the case goes to final judgment and we have omitted an important claim or defense, the broadened rules of claim preclusion will foreclose us from coming up with a different theory on which to litigate.

No matter how many years you have spent in the law, you have witnessed an impressive number of instances in which legal rules have grown or shrunk to permit or cut off claims. The borderland between contract and tort has been shifted. Product liability law has expanded. Defenses to negligence actions have disappeared or been limited in various ways. The litigation over private rights of action for all sorts of regulatory and statutory violations continues.

In the arena of human rights, where I have done battle from time to time, the list of actionable wrongs has grown as the principle of accountability takes hold; a pattern of police beatings can now be seen as battery, infringement of a federal, and state, constitutional right, and more recently as torture forbidden by international conventions and peremptory norms of international law. In this example, the structure of legal rules requires thinking of the given facts in several different ways, and making arguments that appeal to different ideas of justice. Freedom from unwanted harm is the basis of a battery claim. A claim of constitutional violation appeals to our sense that all citizens are entitled to fair treatment, but

requires us to overcome the inevitable police claim of qualified immunity. When we talk about torture, we are discussing
a norm that is born of human struggle and human experience, a norm that came into the transnational legal structure
based on a sense of fundamental human rights that exist irre-
spective of borders. For each of these claims, we will be asking the jurors to think about related but different ideas and
bases of justice.

Beyond substantive law, legal rules about procedure and
evidence critically determine how you will present your case.
You must internalize and act upon these rules. One example
suffices. In a family court case, the wife had called the police
during a domestic dispute and the police officer had witnessed some of the husband's violent acts. The wife's counsel
offered the police report in evidence. Objection: hearsay. Sustained, under the applicable law in that jurisdiction. The next
day, the wife's counsel called the police officer and asked him
if he had prepared the report. "Yes," the officer said. Counsel
offered the report. Objection: hearsay. Sustained, although
there is an argument for admissibility in a civil case.

The point is that counsel had not troubled to think
through how the rules of evidence would limit the varieties
of admissible proof. Indeed, the police officer's testimony
would probably have been more direct and persuasive than a
written report could ever be. A reader may be tempted to
think that this example is too basic. Surely all trial lawyers
know the hearsay rule, and this lawyer's failure to understand it must be the exception. Not so, according to the judge
who told me the story.

Another more complex example occurred in a New York federal case involving alleged support for terrorism. Two Yemeni defendants were charged with aiding the violent acts of Al-Qaeda and Hamas. At their trial, the prosecution offered and the court allowed graphic evidence, including testimony and pictures of a Tel Aviv bus bombing with which the defendants had no direct connection. The court of appeals reversed the convictions, holding that the prejudicial and cumulative effect of this evidence far outweighed its probative value, particularly given the emotionally charged environment of a terrorism case in New York in the first decade of the twenty-first century.

The prosecutors who offered this evidence had a good idea that the judge would probably admit it, and that the jury would find it dramatic and persuasive. The prosecutors forgot that the Supreme Court has specifically cautioned against the use of unduly graphic and marginally relevant evidence in criminal cases. In short, they stepped outside the structure of legal rules—in this case, rules about evidence—that must confine the process of trial.

There are reasons why lawyers sometimes have tunnel vision, instead of the broad appreciation of the historical, social, and cultural context in which issues arise. One reason is the changing nature of legal research.

I believe that present-day legal research and legal education harm our ability to see the structure of legal rules, and the relationship of those rules to their social, cultural, and historical setting. Westlaw and Lexis and other computer-based legal research tools are valuable, but they are designed to narrow your vision. They work best when you already have decided on a tentative answer to your problem. Having that answer in mind, you use words you already know to formulate a search query. That query spouts back items that use those words. As our search for authority and information becomes more and more focused, we are less and less likely to see context.

Students and lawyers seem bent on finding "the rule," or "the case with the rule." Rules thus acquire a disembodied reality. They are reified rather than being seen in relationship to processes that occur in historical time. Richard Delgado and Jean Stefancic have written on this theme, and their work—cited in the Notes—repays study.

In the first year of law school, we all took basic courses. We were to learn techniques of reasoning, and the way that these themes of legal reasoning arose in time, developed, and related to one another in a given social system. At least, I hope we were doing that, rather than worrying about "hornbook rules" and "what will be on the exam." When we see a client story, we should reflect on the injustice of the client's situation by recalling all the ways in which that story might be told. We should begin with the broadest possible approach. We must be open even to implausible theories and ideas that might turn out to serve our purpose. We should see the categories and structure of legal thought as supple, interrelated, and perhaps open to new content. Only then can we descend to a reality check and decide on a case strategy and theme.

To put the matter in terms of Westlaw and Lexis searches, we need to figure out imaginative and intelligent questions before we can obtain truly useful answers. A few years ago, the legal writing instructors at the University of Texas divided first-year students into two groups. Those in the first group were to do all their research on computer-based systems. Those in the the second group were prohibited from using the computer until they had browsed in the library, studied books and articles, with special attention to works that were not simply handbooks. The second group eventually found 45 percent more useful authority in its research than the first group.

Delgado and Stefancic recall Edgar Allen Poe's story, "The Murders in the Rue Morgue," one of those cases in which homicides took place under seemingly impossible conditions. Impossible, that is, until a brilliant investigator with an open mind surveyed all the possible means by which the crime could have been committed and came up with the right answer. He refused to be confined by the artificial structure of thought imposed by officialdom, and adopted a structure that took account of what might have been and not simply what was thought probable.

In our law practice, we are sometimes like those doctors who see ten patients an hour and make lightning diagnoses, usually with a quick prescription that will deal with the symptom they have identified. Other physicians criticize that method of practice, and it demonstrably enhances the chance of error.

Yet, in our law practices, how often have we listened for a short while to a client or a witness and then pigeonholed that story as "another one of those" x, or y, or z tales that we have heard. And then, with that lightning diagnosis, we have fit the story into one of the learned and narrow structures upon which we habitually rely. Or perhaps we listen, consider briefly, do some focused research, and give an "answer," with "reasons" and "analysis," as we were taught in legal writing class. Under the pressure enhanced by instant communication and our busy schedules, we don't take time to stop and think about the broader structures of law and fact into which the story might fit. This recital shows the way that structure, observation, rapport, and skepticism all fit together in our work.

Structure of Your Team

When I take a case, I think about the team we will need to handle it. Some years ago, I rejoined a law firm where I had practiced. The firm had grown and changed. A partner who had not been there on my earlier tour of duty asked me to take over a complex case, in which our client was being sued for libel, trade libel, and violation of the antitrust law. He began by saying that I could have 25 percent of this associate's time, 50 percent of that associate's time, and so on. I demurred politely. No, I said, I want one associate to run the case with me, and the assurance that his and my secretaries—each of whom had litigation experience—would function as paralegals on the case. I thought we could maneuver toward summary judgment and if we did not win at that stage or settle the case, we might think of adding someone to a trial team. My next move was to hire an expert witness on a key issue, to help us develop a summary judgment and trial plan. I then set up a meeting with the client, including the people who had been most involved in the activity and publication that led to the lawsuit. I wanted them to meet the team, and to understand the roles they were to play. I also wanted to give the necessary warning that they were not to talk about the case among themselves, but to communicate with the lawyers if they had something to contribute. This warning is even more important in a criminal matter.

I was appointed in a federal capital case. Before taking the appointment, I told the judge that I must have freedom to choose co-counsel, hire additional lawyers if necessary and to choose paralegals and investigators. I also brought in a team of law students early on, and some of them stayed with the case to the end.

When you imagine your team, I reiterate that an investigator on the street early in the case can save time, expense, and trouble later on. Many lawyers think first of discovery devices when they think about the facts. This is a mistake that can be costly.

A large corporation hired me to be lead counsel in litigation. They had lost a case in federal district court and there was going to be an appeal. However, the victorious plaintiff's firm had filed a class action based on the initial case, seeking to multiply its success by more than one thousand. That same firm filed in federal and state court on the same group of claims. Then, a group of plaintiffs represented by a different firm filed a related case in federal court in another state. How did the team approach work?

First, I was to be lead counsel. Somebody has to be the leader, and the client must confirm his or her authority. An institutional client must choose someone—an empowered liaison—to work with that lead lawyer. That person must have plenary authority, or at least access to somebody who can make quick decisions on major issues. I was at that point a solo lawyer, so we needed a law firm to do the heavy lifting. However, I insisted that the chosen law firm field a team built along the principles that I discuss above. We then needed local lawyers in each of the two jurisdictions where trial court litigation was pending.

The client at first wanted to get a large law firm in each of those jurisdictions. I foresaw difficulties of coordination, as well as unnecessary expense. We selected "boutique" litigation firms in each of the two locations, and within those firms chose one or two lawyers we wanted to work with. We fielded an efficient and effective team.

It is not enough to think of a team. How will the team work? Every team member must be aware of the entire case story. They will all do their best work if they regularly meet by phone or in person, assign tasks, report on progress, and share ideas. Once upon a time, it would not be necessary to say these things. However, with much litigation becoming complex, and with the advent of email and voice mail, law practice is changing. I mentioned this issue briefly in the section on Rapport.

Too often, senior lawyer sends a request to paralegal or associate by email and gets a response. Perhaps the associate drafts a pleading, which the senior lawyer then marks up with the word-processing program and sends back. Exchange of ideas is twice truncated in this process—first by limiting the form of communication and second by not involving the team in the exercise. The preparation effort suffers and the learning curve for younger lawyers and other participants is stultified.

I also see cases in which a senior lawyer is briefed by the juniors for a trial appearance or oral argument, without having been a party to all the work that went into preparing for that presentation. The senior lawyer's superior advocacy skills cannot make up for the relative lack of depth of his or her knowledge of the case.

In difficult cases, two or three lawyers may be "in charge," each contributing strengths to the team. It is important to establish lines of authority and responsibility. Again, I have seen teams in which one lawyer is doing the "stand up" work, yet will not take the time to understand what everyone on the team is doing. This is not delegation of responsibility, it is abdication of a nondelegable duty.

I have heard many stories of corporate clients who put limits on lawyer billings in ways that discourage the kind of team-building of which I speak. They will not pay for lawyer time spent in conference with other lawyers. They audit bills in ways that encourage parceling out lawyer and paraprofessional tasks in fragmentary ways. Sometimes these dictates are at the level of "policy" and are hard to overcome. I think such limitations are short-sighted and, in fact, based on a false sense of cost-effectiveness. In addition, if the corporation is an insurance company retaining counsel to defend the insured, the company must be reminded that the insured is the client and is owed a duty of effective defense.

Team effort, over the long term, is more efficient. It produces better settlements and trial results. I base this conclusion on having led litigation teams and having read and written about complex litigation for decades. The law firm faced with these issues should be prepared with a litigation budget that shows how the team method saves client money and produces better work. Consider where the cost of billing team conferences can be offset: for example, use of informal discovery, less churning of paperwork by lower-level associates and paraprofessionals who are not in the loop and therefore do not function as effectively as they should, consolidation of tracking functions, using the techniques discussed in Chapter Six. The team method forces the lead counsel to be involved early and more intensely in case preparation than is often the case. Some lead lawyers take the case and then let lower-level partners and associates "work it up." The lead lawyer then steps in for trial or the last push toward settlement. This form of practice is said to maximize the lead lawyer's availability to jump around from potential trial to potential trial. In my experience, the resulting lack of leadership runs up the bills unnecessarily.

If a law firm dares to challenge some of the received wisdom about team-building, it may initially find that it cannot bill lawyer time as it wishes. Over time, however, the firm should be able to demonstrate that its method works better than the alternative.

Structure of Evidence Rules

Every trial lawyer must wear the rules of evidence like a cloak. The rules of evidence may be grouped as those dealing with relevance and its counterweights (such as undue prejudice and repetition), truth-seeking and its counterweights (such as privilege and legality), the adversary system limitation on hearsay (with the many exceptions, rooted in various policies), and so on. I speak of this metaphorical garb for several practical reasons having to do with the nature of evidence rules in trials.

- Cases are rarely reversed for error in admitting or excluding evidence, therefore many potential objections are optional.
- A lawyer may want to let something in, even though an objection could be made, to accomplish some trial goal.
- While motions in limine can be litigated before trial, and evidence issues briefed during trial, almost all evidentiary objections and responses are spur-of-the-moment things; there is no time to look up a potential objection and then formulate it.

These days, almost all jurisdictions have adopted either an Evidence Code (as in California), or some version of the Federal Rules of Evidence. Learning the code sections or rule numbers is no substitute for knowing the structure of evidence rules; the codification movement has helped us to understand structure by grouping rules in meaningful categories.

When you imagine the trial story, you must picture the testimony of each witness, and the content of each exhibit, evaluating them for admissibility. In resisting the opponent's case, you must decide which motions in limine you will file to secure pretrial evidence rulings. Pretrial motions practice is indispensable. Rulings will prevent your giving an opening statement about matter that the jurors will not be permitted to see. They may prevent your opponent from tossing a skunk into the jury box that cannot be removed even when the evidence behind the allegation turns up missing.

Structure of the Case Plan

Another name for this topic could be "structure of procedure." The phrase "trial notebook" is helpful but incomplete. From the moment you take a case, you must develop a plan of action that carries you though pretrial action, trial preparation, and trial. Some clients want a litigation budget. Even if the client does not demand such a thing, every lawyer and law firm must create a budget for each case. Litigation involves investment decisions, in which time and money will be expended in search of a result.

"Result" often cannot be measured in dollars. Child custody decisions, enforcement of human rights, much injunctive relief in general—all of these may require spending time and money.

The case plan respects the principles discussed in these essays, and it defines roles for members of the team. Here is a checklist:

- Does the complaint lay out a plausible theory of the case? Even though the rules permit notice pleading, I believe that a complaint must identify the parties, then contain a paragraph entitled "Nature of This Case." That paragraph is a one- or two-sentence statement of the goals and principles of this litigation, designed to give the reader—trial judge, media, opponent—a sense of the case. It is what you would say to a friend who asks, "What is your case about?" I do not advocate prolixity, but the complaint should tell the story in plain English. This complaint helps you to formulate the rest of your case plan.

- Based on the client story you have tentatively adopted, what testimony and exhibits will you need? Use the tools described in Chapter Six.

- Investigation, written discovery, oral discovery: This is the most efficient and effective order of factual preparation. Assign team members to these tasks and have a timeline for finishing them. Seek an early discovery conference with the judge, if your jurisdiction does not do that as a matter of course. Your objective is to find the facts, and to control discovery usage before it becomes diffuse and expensive.

- Research, motions practice, jury instructions, in limine: This is the proper order of law-based work. Despite my skepticism about most threshold-of-litigation motions, you will need to examine issues of subject-matter jurisdiction (particularly in federal court), personal jurisdiction, and substantive sufficiency of the complaint. In particular areas of law, federal and state legislatures have imposed pleading and other requirements that must be considered at the outset of the case. If you are suing a public official, or representing one being sued, immunity issues will arise immediately. And in federal court there are the venerable standing, mootness, and political question doctrines to contend with. As an initial matter, you must examine your case to see where partial or complete summary judgment will be appropriate. In a criminal case, pretrial motions test the government's legal theory and the legality of its evidence. These legal issues present you with ways to shape the case for settlement or trial. Strike as early as you have something potentially useful to say to the court. This activist posture toward the litigation pays dividends. As your team fills in the structure of your case with facts and law, you can craft motions in limine that will control the conduct of trial. Create a file of memoranda on legal, procedural, and evidentiary points. From this file, you can create memos to file during trial.

- When trial comes, you will choose the members of the team who will be in court and those who will be working back at the office. Again, the team approach can help you. I do respect some jury consultants, and I advocate using jury questionnaires. But I have also found that every member of the team, if they have worked on the case in the way I advocate, has something useful to contribute to jury selection. They have insights into the attitudes and behavior of prospective jurors. Lead counsel have the deciding role, but listening to team members pays off.

- At trial, the team must be seen to work in harmony, as I have noted before.
- As I noted above, your file of legal points will come in handy at trial. You will be able to file short, persuasive memoranda on disputed evidence points, and written support for your argument on motions at the close of the plaintiff's case and when all the evidence is in. You will be able to participate more effectively in settling the jury instructions that will be given.

We can see this set of "structure" tasks from a different but equally revealing perspective. The client tells the story to reflect his or her view of experiences, and his or her sense of injustice. Your job must be to rearrange the client's narrative, and fill out its details, in ways that fit the legal categories and rules of evidence. Example: The client has killed her spouse. She shows symptoms of mental illness. She speaks of justification for the killing—her husband was unfaithful and abusive. This is a compelling story. She poses no risk of recidivism. The narrative, however, must be fitted into legal categories that accomplish several results. First, you seek to maximize the prospect of little or no punishment. Second, you seek a legal theory that gives the maximum chance to give the jury the entire story of her situation; you read the statutes and judicial interpretation and make choices.

The killing seems to have been intentional, or at least claiming otherwise would not pass the straight-face test. One cannot plausibly say that the gun went off by accident. Her conduct was not the result of automatism or somnambulism or some other condition that negates the existence of a voluntary act.

You are therefore limited to thinking about murder, the mental element of which varies depending on what jurisdiction you are in, and voluntary manslaughter, which is a form of intentional homicide done in heat of passion or under extreme emotional distress, again depending on what state's penal code is applicable.

Voluntary manslaughter can give you a verdict that might result in a sentence of probation, but so lenient a sentence is unlikely. You keep looking. You turn to the law of excuse, which includes insanity. You find that in the wake of John Hinckley's acquittal by reason of insanity for shooting Ronald Reagan, all states have narrowed the definition of insanity and imposed more or less onerous burdens of proof on defendants who raise the defense. In addition, a verdict of not guilty by reason of insanity can lead to "civil commitment," which can be a longer and harsher result than jail.

You remain troubled because you want to introduce mental-condition evidence that helps the jury see why your client's conduct was not morally blameworthy. So you look at the law's idea of justification, which points in this case to self-defense. However, your client was not under any immediate threat of deadly harm. You do more research and find that many states, including your own, have recognized that in the context of conjugal violence the abused spouse may raise a justification defense for killing the abuser. The same words are being used, but with a broader content. And, you also find, expert testimony supplemented by lay testimony may be admissible.

You devise a structure of themes for your case, and put elements of the client's narrative into the structure at the appropriate places, backed up with physical and testimonial evidence. I give some other examples of this process elsewhere in this chapter.

When a client brings you a civil case, you soon face difficult issues of structure. Under which legal theories will you bring the case? If there are state and federal claims, will you bring them all in federal court, in state court if this is possible, or will you divide the case into two parts and file in two forums? You must choose a forum where you will have personal jurisdiction, and if you are too aggressive in your choice, you condemn yourself to needless litigation on "minimum contacts." Each potential forum has its own structures of pleading, procedure, and evidence. A federal forum may give you a jury of six while a state court jury will be twelve. The state court jury is drawn from one county, the federal jury from an entire judicial district. All of these structures are relatively fixed and inevitable, and you should obviously make your choices consciously and not by default.

Structure of the Courtroom Space

The first time I saw Edward Bennett Williams in court, he had an FBI clerk on the stand who had been subpoenaed to describe the FBI's illegal electronic surveillance of a hotel room with a spike mike inserted in the baseboard from an adjoining room. There was no jury. Williams began his examination from the back of the courtroom, and as he asked questions of the increasingly nervous agent, he stepped forward toward the witness box a small pace at a time. When the witness became visibly upset, the prosecutor objected and the judge asked Williams to step back. He did, but by taking backward steps a little at a time, asking questions all the while.

I sat in wonder. He had a mental picture of the courtroom, so that he could move forward and back at will. He punctuated his questions by stepping forward, leaning toward the witness. He used subtle body language to convey doubt or curiosity to hear more.

I am concerned with sight-lines in the courtroom. I want the jury to have a good view of our table and of our client. I do not want their view blocked by opposing counsel's position or wanderings. I take seriously Terry MacCarthy's warning that lawyers should not hover behind the lectern unless ordered to do so. Move out from behind it. Make sure the jurors can see exhibits easily and without distraction from what else is going on in the courtroom.

The great Ann Richards, governor of Texas, used to tell a story about growing old. "Somebody asked me the other day, 'Do you believe in the hereafter?' I said, 'Of course I do. I go from room to room in my house saying to myself, "Now what am I here after?"'"

When you are moving in the courtroom, you must always be asking yourself that question. Your movements should have a purpose related to persuasion. Too many lawyers move randomly, betraying nervousness, or unintentionally misdirecting the observer who wonders why the lawyer is wandering around, or using jerky hand gestures. You say to yourself, "I will begin my opening statement at the lectern, but walk over and put my hand on my client's shoulder." Or, "I will turn and look at my client." Or, "I will make eye contact with somebody in the audience who may be called as a witness, knowing the jurors will follow my gaze." You may want to stand farther from the jury as you begin your opening, then take a step or two toward the jury box a few minutes later. Your movements may communicate intense interest, disbelief, a need for further elaboration. But all of them must relate to your primary purpose.

Your movements must be economical. A courtroom is a small space, compared to a tent show or political rally. The space within which you communicate with the jurors, and examine witnesses, is smaller yet. Your gestures must fit the space. As you think about the structure of argument and examination, imagine yourself doing these things in the physical structure where these events will take place.

Structure of Opening Statement

I used to preach just one approach to the structure of opening statement, and I continue to believe that it is right for most cases. However, I have studied other approaches used by winning lawyers, and I will share those with you as well. One rule remains absolute and inviolable. You must have a structure, that is, a way of organizing your opening that you have decided upon deliberately and that you can justify to yourself and other members of your team.

I don't like to rehearse jury or judge argument. However, I always share at least the structure and main ideas of the opening with the team.

You know everything about your case. The jurors know nothing, except what little gleanings they have from the judge's initial comments and voir dire. If the case has generated media attention, the jurors may think they know something about it, but almost certainly they do not. Even if the case has been covered in the media, and the jurors do know a lot about it, they are supposed to start with a clean slate. This is a fiction, of course, but what they think they know is probably not what you want them to think they know. The evidence will almost inevitably come in piece by piece; jurors need a framework within which to accept and use that which they see and hear.

Opening statement is your opportunity to "say your case." If you represent a defendant, you will not put on evidence for a while except through cross-examination. Even if you are the plaintiff, the evidence will not come in as a "story." The jurors need a place to "put" each item of evidence as they hear or see it.

It is easy to forget this lesson. We see lawyers who jump right into the middle of their facts in opening statement. We see this error repeated when they do direct examination, and don't give enough background. We see it also on cross-examination, when they give no hint of why these questions are being asked.

If you are permitted to use exhibits in opening statement, do so sparingly. This is your chance to create a relationship with the jury and a multimedia presentation will not permit you to do that. In direct and cross-examination, and in closing argument, I advocate using exhibits extensively. In witness examination, exhibits help to create impressions that jurors will retain, beyond simply remembering what a witness says. In closing argument, exhibits help empower the jurors to review the evidence. However, opening statement is your first opportunity to look at the jurors and establish a relationship of confidence and trust. In jurisdictions that allow lawyer voir dire, you will have met the jurors, but now they are in the seats they will occupy to listen to the evidence. They have been sworn for this case. They form a new collective body. You don't want to use props that obscure you and your message. "Sparingly" does not mean none or never. It simply means that you must see opening statement in its relationship to the other parts of the trial.

If you are the plaintiff, you begin by making eye contact with jurors. Then you say "May it please the Court, counsel, [name of client], members of the jury." I prefer "members of the jury" to "ladies and gentlemen."

Next, tell the jury what this case is about, in one or two sentences. Say your story, the one that was the "nature of this case" paragraph in your complaint. "This case is about Mary Smith [indicating], who is a qualified legal secretary, and who needed her job. And it is about John Jones, who made her life at work unbearable by making crude and unwanted sexual advances."

Next, introduce yourself and your team. "My name is Paula Winston, and with the other members of our team, we are going to present the evidence that proves what I just said. The other people on our team, who you will see here in court working on the case, are …" The jurors want to know who is helping you and who will have what job.

Then, acknowledge and embrace your burden of proof. "We brought this case. We have the burden of proving to you what we say. We embrace that burden." Notice you do not say that "this opening statement is not evidence," or any such self-deprecating thing. "In this opening statement, I am going to outline the facts we are going to prove. After I tell you the basic 'elements' of our case, my discussion falls into the three main areas that the proof will reveal." I say "three." Triplets—things in threes—are provably easier to recall. If you can, use triplets in argument and examination. Here, your triplets might be, "First, I want to talk about Mary Smith, who she is and how she qualified for a job with John Jones. Second, I want to talk about what happened to Mary Smith when she began work with John Jones."

Notice we are calling people by their first and last names. You know her as Mary, but in court she has a last name and she is Mary Smith or Ms. Smith. "Third, I will tell you all the ways in which Mary Smith was harmed, for, as we said in voir dire, when we prove our case it becomes necessary to figure what sum of money in damages will put Mary Smith back where she would have been without this wrongful conduct, and, if you make the findings we contend the evidence requires, what these defendants should have to pay in punitive damages." If liability and damages are bifurcated, or more likely if the punitive damages aspect is bifurcated, you obviously don't introduce it in that way, but tell the jury that there will be two phases. The 1-2-3 is, therefore, client, what happened, and how the jurors can make it right.

Now, tell the jury the elements of the case—the items that must be proved in order to have a verdict in your favor. This is an "outline" of the case, based on the pretrial order. It is also a chance for you to say, as you list these things, what is and is not disputed. In other writing, I have referred to "the theory of minimal contradiction." Your story diverges from the other side's story only enough to require a verdict in your favor. You don't take on the burden of proving more than is necessary to win your case.

In telling the story of your case, you have choices of structure. You want to choose the element of the story that resonates most strongly with the jurors. For years, I have used the 1-2-3 image, making the story of the case No. 2. I now realize that this may not be helpful. I have made many opening statements, and the 1-2-3 approach has helped me. But the reader may well ask, "How should I organize the No. 2? Does it make a difference how I arrange the story?"

The answer is, "of course it makes a difference." From Aristotle on forward, we understand the importance of "arrangement" in our presentation. I know this from experience, but have not adequately explained it. I am like the character in Molière's play who says, "Par ma foi! Il y a plus de quarante ans que je dis de la prose sans que j'en susse rien." My goodness, for forty years, I have been speaking prose without knowing it!

No formula, not even my proposed one, will be right for

every case. Sometimes you will begin opening statement with a scene-setting paragraph or two, and then move into the essential business of introducing the team, outlining the issues, and previewing the proof in a memorable way. In an air-crash case, plaintiff's counsel began by playing an excerpt from the cockpit voice recorder as the airplane approached the airport. "At that moment," counsel continued, "Harry Johnson did not know that he had only three minutes to live."

There are elements of every story that belong in first place because they engage the jurors and make them ready to accept the rest of your portrayal of events. Take, for example, the Vioxx litigation. More than 10,000 plaintiffs sued Merck, claiming that they were harmed or that their loved ones died from using Vioxx, marketed as a pain reliever. A coalition of plaintiffs' lawyers on one side and Merck lawyers on the the other side set cases for trial. After about a dozen trials, the parties began serious work on a global settlement, a process discussed in Chapter Two.

It is instructive to review how lawyers in these cases arranged the "story" part of their opening statements. In a wrongful-death case tried in Texas state court, plaintiff's lawyer Mark Lanier began by briefly telling the jurors that the case would call upon them to be like "CSI," and to figure out just how the plaintiff's decedent died. He then turned to his main opening theme. Once upon a time, Merck was a responsible company directed by scientists. Then it came under new management devoted to increasing profitability. These new managers ignored warning signs that the scientists within and without the company had raised about the dangers of Vioxx. In short, Merck made decisions about danger to human life based on dollars. Lanier was telling the jury that there would be compelling evidence of a motive to get Vioxx to market before all issues of its potential safety were resolved. This was not only the strongest part of Lanier's case, but a powerful theme in many product-liability cases. Juries are uncomfortable with private profit-centered corporations calculating risks and benefits about products with a potential to do harm. Lanier won his case.

In another Vioxx case, defense lawyer Philip Beck started his opening by saying:

> Thank you, Your Honor. Mr. Birchfield [plaintiff's counsel] talked for about sixty minutes. While he was talking, about sixty people across the United States died from exactly the same thing that caused Mr. Irvin's death and not a single one of them was taking Vioxx. I'm going to talk for about sixty minutes, and while I'm talking another sixty people across the United States will die of the same thing that caused Mr. Irvin's death, and not a single one of them is taking Vioxx. The reason is that the thing that caused Mr. Irvin's death is the leading cause of death in the United States of America. That was true before Vioxx ever came on the market, and that's true today after Vioxx is no longer being sold. Several hundred thousand people a year die from having arteries that are clogged up with plaque, then having a rupture in the plaque, and then having a blood clot form in the artery so

that not enough blood gets to the heart. It's the leading cause of death in the United States.

Beck focused on the issue of causation, which on the defense side is often the main issue in a product liability case. His client won.

In your case, how will you choose where to start? What images will you deploy? First, your chosen images must resonate with the jury to whom you are speaking. Some lawyers use focus groups to help identify those images. I am not a fan of expensive and lengthy mock trials. Rather, if one is to use a consultant, do a sort of combined opening and closing on videotape, and have the consultant show it to some people who the consultant knows how to select.

In most cases, there will not be the budget to hire consultants. Some great lawyers never use them. In any event, the duty of picking the images and arrangement for the opening is the lawyer's and is not delegable. I recall speaking at the Texas Bar Association luncheon some years ago in Fort Worth. Steve Susman was another speaker, and he described using consultants in trial preparation. Joe Jamail, the larger-than-life trial lawyer who won Pennzoil-Texaco, strode to the microphone as the next speaker and intoned, "Steve, I would rather have a boil on my ass than use a trial consultant."

In the Vioxx cases, the image of a defendant motivated by greed has emotive power that can carry the jury over difficulties in other parts of the proof. The problem of causation brings jurors back to the rules by which the case is to be decided. The tension between emotive and rule-based discourse lurks in every case. Another example, from an entirely different area of law, is the Santa Barbara, Calif., prosecution of singer Michael Jackson in 2005. Jackson was charged with molesting a minor child and related offenses. The prosecution used liberal California evidence law to bring in extensive evidence of Jackson's alleged improprieties with other children, his unusual and allegedly perverted fascination with children, and other activities that the prosecution thought would portray Jackson as a depraved stalker of young people and unworthy of belief. The defense kept its focus on the issue of what happened between Jackson and the alleged victim, and the motivations of those summoned to testify for the prosecution. The jury rejected the prosecution effort to divert attention from the main issue and acquitted Jackson.

When you choose the arrangement of the story, begin by focusing on the element or elements that you will stress every day and with as many witnesses as possible.

As you tell the story, introduce the witnesses, letting the jurors know why they will be here. No need to introduce all the witnesses—too much detail bogs the story down. For example: "You are going to hear about the kinds of comments that John Jones made to Mary Smith starting the first week she was on the job. One witness will be Anthony Parsons, the secretary who sits at the desk closest to where Mary Smith was sitting. He was able to see and hear better than anybody. And he will tell you …"

If there are problems with your evidence, tell the jury about them. "Now I want to be fair about this. Mary Smith is not perfect. You are going to hear that when she gets frightened or upset, she … "

If the plaintiff's opening is usually 1-2-3, the defendant's opening will usually be 2-1-3. That is, the defendant must acknowledge the event that brings us all to this courtroom, then talk about the client and the result. I did this in opening for Terry Nichols.

> May it please the Court, Counsel, Mr. Nichols, members of the jury, on the nineteenth morning of April at 9:02 in the morning, or actually just a few minutes before, Timothy McVeigh parked in front of the Murrah Building in Oklahoma City. He was in a Ford F-700 truck from Ryder Rentals with a 20-foot box. And Timothy McVeigh was not alone. With him in the cab of that truck were one or two other people. The driver parked the truck and set the bomb to go off.

> Yes, Terry Nichols was not there and did not know about the bombing until the next day. He was at home in Herington, Kans., at 109 South 2d Street in a house he'd bought and moved into one month and six days before. He was at home. With him there were his pregnant wife, Marife; their infant daughter, Nicole; Marife Torres Nichols, born in the Philippines, who came to the United States as Terry Nichols' wife. Terry Nichols was building a life, not a bomb.

> My name is Michael Tigar; and with our team, I represent Terry Nichols. We're here to gain respect for the undeniable fact that right now Terry Nichols is presumed

innocent. We're here to help point out the hundreds of reasonable doubts that lurk in the evidence.

In this opening statement, I want to introduce you first to our team members, the ones that are going to help us here; and then I want to outline for you the allegations, the charges, to point out what is not in dispute, what we agree with these prosecutors about, and what on the other hand we do contest, what the government will try to prove and fail, and where you may find the reasonable doubts when the evidence is all in. Yes, when the evidence is all in.

Can you see my hand? You can't see my hand. Not until I've turned it over and showed you both sides could you say that you've seen my hand. And just as in life, the last bit of evidence about an important thing may be the thing that lights up the whole picture, so we beg you to have open minds. We'll present evidence to you, beginning with our cross-examination of the very first witnesses that take that witness stand; but for the first few weeks of the trial, the government has the choice of what witnesses to bring, what evidence to bring. He that pleadeth his cause first seemeth just, but the defendant come and searcheth it out.

Over and over again, you're going to hear about the presumption of innocence. That means we start with a clean page. That means that suspicion, prejudice, prejudgment, speculation have no place.

Now, when the government rests, we are going to present our witnesses and exhibits. So after introduc-

tions and review of the allegations here, Ron Woods and
I, my co-counsel, are going to do an opening statement in
three parts so that you can have a perfect way of keeping track of the strands of proof.

There are some other principles that apply particularly
to defendants.

Talk about why the evidence will not support these
claims that are being made here. Even if you are defending a
criminal case, it is not enough to say that the plaintiff will not
sustain its burden of proof. No, you must present a plausible
alternative reality, and tell the jury that you are not assuming
a burden of proof that you do not have, but rather give this
alternative version to to shine a light on the gaps in your
opponent's proof.

Do not use opening statement to get into a fight with
your opponent. Assume that your opponent has chosen the
strongest ground on which to fight—for their side. If you join
them on that ground, you take an unnecessary risk. Your
opening is designed not only to tell the story, but to choose
the terms in which the story will be told. Set out your story
as a free-standing and independent structure. I can recall
reading a product-liability trial transcript. Plaintiff's counsel
attacked the manufacturer for greed, carelessness in product
testing, undue haste in getting the product to market, and,
finally, the alleged causal link between the product and the
plaintiff's husband's death. The first three items were strong
talking points with emotional appeal. Defense counsel's
opening took the same four points in the same order, leaving

causation to the last. Yet causation was the defense's strongest point. The lesson: Know your strengths and play to them. Talk to the jurors about the reasons they should keep an open mind until all the evidence is in. Look at the excerpt from Edward Bennett Williams opening in Chapter Eight.

And always, no matter what side you are on, tell the jury what you want them to do. Tell them you will ask for their verdict, and what—at least in general terms—you want that verdict to be.

Structure of Direct Examination

Direct examination, as practiced, is often boring and formless. Civil lawyers are accustomed to doing depositions. Judge Bill Wilson once wrote to lawyers in a case that their presentation of an expert looked more like a deposition than a structured direct and cross. That was about the most damning criticism that he could conjure up. Of all the aspects of direct examination, structure is perhaps the most important. In part, a lawyer's difficulty arises from the difference between courtroom testimony and daily conversation. The witness cannot simply tell the story. "Narrative" is forbidden. One nonleading question at a time, says the rule, and each answer limited by the rules of evidence concerning hearsay, repetition, opinion, and so on. The witness must speak from personal knowledge; that rule emphasizes the gap between what we "know" and what we are entitled to say we know.

In daily conversation, we usually speak colloquially, even elliptically, leaving out ideas and events that are mutually understood within the group. The testifying witness is talking to jurors who do not yet know the story, and who may not share the witness's perspective and way of describing the world. I refer here to the inherent problem that words are often an inadequate or ambiguous way to project an image of some past event. Your direct examination must be detailed enough that the jury gets the same mental picture of the described event that the witness has in her mind. There is more on this topic in Chapter Five, in the essay on "Witnesses as Observers."

There are several principles of direct examination organization that will serve you well. James McElhaney speaks of the paragraph theory of direct. As we learned in English class, every paragraph has a topic sentence, and is limited to a single topic. This is important guidance. Paragraphs have varying levels of detail. Some paragraphs describe events over a long period of time. Some paragraphs descend to detail, giving us a rich and full word picture of a person, place, or event. If you think of direct examination as a series of paragraphs, you can accomplish two goals. First, you move as paragraphs do, topic by topic. Second, you will use the differing levels of detail to shape and shade the mental image you want jurors to form.

In *Examining Witnesses*, I advocated the use of three structural devices: "loops," "prologues," and "transitions." All three devices can be used in cross-examination as well as on direct. A loop repeats a part of the last answer to introduce the next question moving: "After the pickup truck ran the stoplight, what happened?" "After he said, 'Would you like to have dinner,' what did he do?" A prologue introduces the themes of a direct examination: "After we talk about what you do for work, I would like to ask you about what you saw on July 15." A transition moves from one topic to another: "Now I want to turn to what you did when you heard Mr. Jones make that remark."

You generously use exhibits in direct examination because they help to structure and guide the pace of dialogue. Exhibits punctuate the dialogue, and they provide important reminders of what the witness said when you sum up at the end of the case. The exhibit might be a document that reflects what the witness is now telling us, a chart, map, picture or diagram, or a physical object associated with the events she is describing.

Structure of Cross-Examination

There are brilliant works on cross-examination. Terry MacCarthy's book is near the top of any list. Francis Wellman's *The Art of Cross-Examination* has much to teach, even though Wellman's reactionary ideology shines through at many points. In my book, *Examining Witnesses*, you may find valuable ideas. Among the rules that govern cross-examination, "have a structure" is the first and perhaps most important. Structure determines the primacy of your main theme, and recency the order of interrogation.

Even in a criminal case, where pretrial discovery is limited, you must have a basic idea of what you can accomplish on cross-examination of each witness before he or she takes the stand. If the answer is "not much," consider foregoing cross-examination of that witness. The jurors expect you to score some points when you stand up; if you can't score, don't start. We must anticipate what the opposing witness will say, and have a tentative structure of cross-examination in mind before he or she testifies. In civil cases, where discovery is more available, we can do more planning.

First, make a file. Collect all prior statements of each witness. Annotate them so you can use them. Think of "statement" broadly, and create a category for "not quite statements." For example, an FBI 302 report of interview is usually not the witness's "statement," though it may contain some quotations from the witness. A police report or investigator's report falls into that same category. But if the witness departs from the version given the investigator in such a report, you may be able to call the investigator. Be aware of versions given by others that contradict what this witness will probably say, so you can nail down the contradiction in order to enhance the testimony of those others when you call them.

Cross-examinations must be structured so that the jury sees exactly what you are doing. You should begin with matter on which you and the witness will agree, or on which the witness can be made to agree. Thus, "We can agree that it was raining?" or, "You are a liar, aren't you?" In the first instance the witness will say yes. In the second, the witness may disagree, leading to a series of questions showing the demonstrable and admitted lies the witness has told. Moving first to the areas of agreement sets a tone, and may induce the witness to have a sense of security about the examination. Also, remember the theory of minimal contradiction. You are seeking to open up just that amount of difference between competing versions that dictates a different result.

If you have doubts whether you have all the witness's prior statements, clear them up. "You were interviewed by Arnold Witkin, the insurance investigator. Is that right? How many times?" Prior statements is a broad concept. They include not only verbatim utterances but also statements made to others, such as investigators or friends. This counsel is particularly important in criminal cases, where the right to pretrial discovery is more limited than in civil cases, and prosecutorial withholding of prior statements is a frequent and significant problem. If the witness diverges from such a prior statement, you may be able to call that other witness and impeach. At least, reminding the witness of the prior statement may improve the witness's answers—from your point of view.

> "Do you remember talking to Arnold Witkin, the investigator, back in December?"
>
> "Yes, I think so."
>
> "You talked to him about where the red car was just after the crash?"
>
> "Do you remember telling him the car was up on the curb?"

This line of questioning can go in any of several directions from here, because you will have established a foundation to offer evidence of hearsay statements not usually admissible for the truth of the matter asserted (because the prior statement was not under oath); at least you will have accomplished the nonhearsay value of contradiction. If the matter is important enough, the rules of evidence may permit you to call Witkin.

Once the preliminaries are out of the way, respect the canon of structure by announcing what you are going to do. "I want to ask you about the telephone calls you made on the evening of April 15, 1995, and then about some of the working conditions there at XYZ Corporation." This is for the jurors' benefit.

When you cross-examine, show the witness documents and objects that bolster your case and make the witness look at them. If these are in evidence, they do not need to be the witness's documents. You can publish documents to the jury by asking the witness to read them, or portions of them.

> "I am showing you what has been admitted under the pretrial order as Defendant's RR [a telephone company record]. Here is page fifteen. Will you look at that and just read to the jury the third telephone call on that page. You made that call, right?"

> You now have the telephone call linked to a record.

> "You called Ms. Smith?"

> "You called her at 6:15 p.m. and you talked for thirty-seven minutes?"

> "And you talked about what she was going to say about Mr. Jones?"

"That was on April 15?"

"On Sept. 19, 1995, you were interviewed by an investigator named Neil Bellows? You told him that you did not talk to Ms. Jones that evening?"

Get out the investigator report. Have it in front of you. Using Fed. R. Evid. 612, take the witness over the inconsistencies, refreshing recollection as you go. If this is not collateral, and the witness will not give you the needed answer, make sure you have the inconsistency clearly in mind and ask:

"Do you deny that you said that?"

"On your oath?"

"But you don't deny that it happened?"

Because cross-examination is a process of extracting good from someone who has been put up there to harm your case, and because you are limited by the principle of immanence, cross-examination is said to require control of the witness. Control is important for two reasons: First, the witness has already hurt you. He or she has gone through all the harmful details of a story. You should exercise control, in order not to invite or permit him or her to repeat. Control provides structure. In addition, as I wrote in *Examining Witnesses*, you cannot get more out of cross-examination than is inherently in it. Cross-examination is about the particular story told by this particular witness.

The witness wants to hurt you. The witness is at least ostensibly against you. Even a neutral observer is cast by the adversary system on one "side" or the other. The abolition of sponsorship and vouching rules does not change the human desire to be seen as right. (Have you ever noticed how the tenor of a friendly "pickup" game of basketball or tennis changes when a couple of people stop to watch the action?) The cross-examiner necessarily challenges "right." The witness looks for chances to reaffirm the right—"Yes, but …" You exercise control to stay in charge.

Your goal is to have a working plurality of jurors say "aha," meaning "we see now the flaws in what this witness has said." Many lawyers do not understand that the "aha" can come at many possible times during trial, and need not even be the result of cross-examination. The jurors can choose to discredit a witness because of what some other witness has said, or based on other evidence; effective lawyer argument shows the contradiction and points to the right result.

The "aha" needn't occur while the witness is on the stand. Trying to make it appear may lead you to take excessive risks. The main purpose of cross may be to lay the basis for closing argument, where the inconsistencies can be spread out again and made part of the story of the case.

Structure of Closing Argument

Closing argument must have a structure. It is your opportunity to put evidence and legal rules into a context that will permit jurors in deliberation to chart the way toward the result you want. All other considerations are subordinate to this goal. Exaggerated rhetorical flourish, witness-by-witness retelling, aimless attacks on the other side—all of these are your enemies because they are the enemies of persuasion. There is room for emotion and a sense of injustice in summation, but always within the structure you have decided upon. In Chapter Ten, I lay out more detailed ideas about presentation of your summation. Here are some thoughts limited to the issue of structure.

First, do not write out your argument and read it. You might as well fax it in. You want your argument to flow, and to be making eye contact with members of the jury. So we are going to make some notes about argument, and have some key ideas. We are going to know the beginning and the end.

Second, assemble the exhibits you will use in final argument.

Next, establish your summation ideas. Don't worry about the order yet. Just write themes on index cards, so you can rearrange and combine them as you continue preparation. You will see that some topics need separate consideration, even though they are central to your case. For example, if there has been a battle of the experts, you may want to focus separately on how the jury should consider expert testimony, and on the relative merits of the witnesses they have heard. Then, having made your point, you can in the later parts of the summation refer back to expert conclusion. If there has been a difficult witness, for you or against you, that witness's testimony may become a separate theme. Once we have our themes, we do two things. First, we put the notes for each one on a separate page. Then we have a separate bucket file with the exhibits and transcript portions that relate to that theme, for ease of use in actual argument.

Themes vary so much depending on the case that it is hard to generalize, but you must introduce the opening by talking about the roles of lawyer, parties, judge, and jurors. You must end by telling the jury exactly what you want.

Now, put your themes in order. You can now see how to combine related ideas into themes, still keeping in mind the idea of minimal contradiction discussed above. Remember how powerful the evidence becomes when you see if from your client's point of view. You are fighting for your story, but now you are about to hand the story to twelve (or six) people who are going to argue about whether it makes sense. You need to equip these jurors to be narrators of your story, to assert its logic, and defend it against alternative versions. All of this is done by sharing with them a point of view, and then taking them through the evidence and the law that justifies taking that point of view. Be sure to capture the central ideas of the judge's instructions on the law. If there have been many mid-trial rulings limiting the purposes for which evidence may be considered, remind the jurors of these; they will probably have forgotten most of them if the trial has been long.

So our summation plan looks like this:

- Introduction—burden of proof, role of the jury, outline of presentation.
- Why we are here—the issue framed in light of our story.
- Before we get to the central issue, there are some things along the way. That is, you may decide to isolate particular trial events, or particular issues about how to evaluate evidence in light of the judge's instructions, and treat

those separately from your main narrative. You may decide to single out one or more key exhibits as a way of underscoring a key point in your story.

- Why the other side can't handle the truth, or why their reality doesn't work. Key flaws in their approach appear here. This is the place to talk about the evidence "they can't explain."

- How we should view the facts, beginning often with a supposition, and moving through the key events from our perspective.

- What do we want the jury to do? Every claim or defense has "elements" that must be proved. Failure of proof gives the opponent the victory. This is true even when the jury is not asked to answer questions or respond to special issues. All civil cases involve damages calculations, which are broken down into categories such as general and special. Sometimes, the "what should the jury do" question is as simple as "guilty" or "not guilty." But in most cases the elements and questions can be confusing to jurors. To give structure to their deliberations and decision, consider using a chart that breaks the decision down into its component parts and suggests an answer to each part. A chart on an easel can do this. In a civil case, you can enlarge a copy of the verdict form and illustrate your argument by writing in the "correct" answers. This will also help to ensure against inconsistent answers that could undo your verdict. Be matter-of-fact as you go through the issues.

When one surveys all the structures within which litigation takes place, one may be tempted to see them as constraints. In one sense they are. Structures of rules limit the permissible ambit of claims and defenses as well as defining and authorizing claims. Structures of evidence limit proof, so that jurors do not overvalue or undervalue testimony and exhibits. But structures also liberate. Properly devised and used, they help ensure that the process is fair and transparent. Structures of procedure define the system within which disputes may be brought and heard. Structures that govern our arguments and examination of witnesses, when properly understood, make us better advocates.

Notes

- Richard Delgado & Jean Stefancic, "Why Do We Tell the Same Stories? Law Reform, Critical Librarianship, and the Triple Helix Dilemma," 42 Stan. L. Rev. 207 (1989); *Why Do We Ask the Same Questions? The Triple Helix Dilemma Revisited, in Legal Information and the Development of American Law: A Collection of Essays in Honor of Robert C. Berring* 146 (Richard A. Danner & Frank G. Houdek eds. 2008).

- I have written about the theory of minimal contradiction and the limits on effective cross-examination in *Examining Witnesses*.

- The Vioxx litigation is discussed in a chapter in *Trial Stories*.

- A brilliant discussion of jury response to issues in a product case is Gary T. Schwartz, "The Myth of the Ford Pinto Case," 43 *Rutgers L. Rev.* 1013 (1991). Schwartz rebuts the "common wisdom" about the Pinto gas tank explosion case by examining the way that the jurors came to see the case. In short, the Pinto case is not so much a lesson about product liability as it is about telling a story and persuading jurors with evidence.

- The Biblical reference in the Nichols opening (he that pleadeth his cause) is an amalgam of several different translations of Proverbs 18:17.
- Ideas about the structure of summation can be seen in *Persuasion: The Litigator's Art*, and in the Professional Education Group reprint of the jury arguments in *U.S. v. Nichols*.

Candor

Your Candor

The next chapter is entitled "Empowerment." When I speak of empowering the jury, and of transparency in trial technique, I advocate an approach to lawyering that treats the jurors as partners in a search for truth, and invites them to be skeptical about lawyer motives and aware of the significance and meaning of trial events. I advocate ways of telling the jurors about how to determine believability, or how to deconstruct an expert opinion, or how to move through exhibits, and evaluate each side's position.

When judges in the courthouse get the idea that you are not candid, they will find ways to make your professional life uncomfortable. That is the career and professional aspect of the matter. A California trial judge put it this way in an interview:

> What are the other things lawyers can do to be effective advocates with the bench besides making winning arguments in their papers? I remember when I was a lawyer, judges always would say, "Remember, your credibility is the most important asset you have

in court." When it was said to me, it was hard for me to see that it was as important as people thought it was. I can now say in bold face, your credibility is the most important asset in court. It is very hard to build, and very easy to lose. The reason it is so important is that judges are always asking themselves, "Whom can I trust?" Judges never have enough time, and they never have as much information as they want. So they're trying to figure out whether the lawyers appearing before them are reliable. Every judge, I believe, wants to make the right decision every single time, and every judge wants to be seen as making the right decision. Not just because of the ego reasons, which are obvious, but also because then the parties will believe they got a fair hearing, which we all know is the most important thing—coming to court and believing you had a fair hearing. So we're constantly asking ourselves, "Whom can I trust? Whom can I not trust? Whose words can I take at face value, and whose must be constantly checked, investigated, and corroborated?"

Candor is more than simply truth-telling. The attitude of candor requires believing in oneself, displaying concern for rational and logical thought. The candid lawyer says in effect, "I have expended time and effort to bring evidence and argument to this process. Trust me."

In Stephen Fry's novel, *The Liar*, a teacher addresses a student:

You write with fluency and conviction, you talk with authority and control. A complex idea here, an abstract proposition there, you juggle with them, play with them, seduce them. There is no movement from doubt to comprehension, no breaking down, no questioning, no excitement. You try to persuade others, never yourself. You recognize patterns, but you rearrange them where you should analyze them. In short, you do not think. You have never thought. You have never said to me anything that you believe to be true, only things which sound true and perhaps even ought to be true: things that, for the moment, are in character with whatever persona you have adopted for the afternoon. You cheat, you short-cut, you lie.

In this passage lurk significant truths about lawyering, and specifically about juror (and public) attitudes toward what lawyers do. If the jurors have the idea that a lawyer is simply rearranging ideas to make them more palatable, as distinct from thinking, evaluating, and believing, they will punish that lawyer with their disapproval. Every case you take to trial must be true and just at some level of generalization, otherwise you would not have accepted the retainer in the first place or would have settled or dismissed the matter somewhere along the line.

Credibility with jurors is won in the same way as with judges. In a jury trial, you hope to start with the jurors being skeptical but ready to believe in your case. Or if there is something about the case that upsets them, you hope they will have confidence that you can and will explain things. In opening statement, you make sure to signal the "bad facts," the uncomfortable aspects of the impending evidence. You don't want the jurors to conclude that you are hiding from the truth. You embrace your burden of proof. You make promises about the evidence, and you keep them.

This is the beginning of Edward Bennett Williams' opening in the trial of former Treasury Secretary John Connally for accepting an unlawful gratuity. He does not simply lay out the evidence that the jurors will hear. He seeks to create a bond of trust. He invites them to have a high expectation of him and the defense team. At the same time, he reminds them that they must also evaluate the other side with the same amount of scrutiny, and to hold the prosecution to its higher burden:

> May it please the court, ladies and gentlemen of the jury:
>
> What Mr. Sale said to you this morning is the opening statement made on behalf of the prosecution. It is a statement of what they hope to prove during the course of this trial, it is not evidence in the case. …
>
> What I say to you now, members of the jury, is a statement of what we confidently expect to demonstrate to you through the testimony of witnesses whom we will call to the stand, through documents and written materials that we will offer in evidence for your inspection.
>
> Now, under the rules of this court, as in every court in the land, the prosecution gets the opportunity to offer

its case first, to call its witnesses and put in such documents and written materials as it chooses to offer which are receivable in evidence.

Not until all of the prosecution's evidence has been laid before you does the opportunity come to the defense to give you its side of this case, and for that reason, right at the outset, I ask you, ladies and gentlemen of the jury, to keep an open mind during the course of this trial, bearing in mind that not until you have heard all of the prosecution's side does the defense have the chance to come forth with its side of the case. …

And so it is with every contested case that is ever tried in this courthouse or any other courthouse in the land, there are two sides. In the ordinary process the prosecution goes first and we come second.

There is one other thing that I would like to say to you right at the outset about opening statements in general made in a court of law. An opening statement by a trial lawyer to a jury is not like a politician's speech. When a politician is seeking office and he makes a speech to people whose votes he is soliciting, he can promise the moon because he doesn't have to deliver on his promises until after the votes are cast, until after the election is over.

But what I say to you this afternoon, members of the jury, in this opening statement, made on behalf of the defendant John Connally in this case, I must deliver on. I must deliver on before you go to your jury room, before you begin your deliberations, before you cast your ballot, because you will hold me responsible for everything I say to you this afternoon when I say that I will prove certain things to you, and well you should.

I welcome that responsibility, because what I say to you this afternoon, members of the jury, in this opening statement made on behalf of the defendant, we shall prove to you through the testimony of witnesses who will take the stand, through documents, and through other written materials that will be offered here before you.

The Other Side's Candor

We have all experienced it: The adversary who says one thing and does another, is economical with the truth, plays games with service of pleadings; in short, who cannot be trusted. Before a jury, this sort of behavior usually gets sorted out fairly quickly and to your adversary's disadvantage. But in the skirmishes before trial, such behavior raises your blood pressure.

We need rules and ideas to guide us when faced with such an adversary. First, don't let this adversary knock you off your case plan. Don't be provoked into doing rash and excessive maneuvers. When you are hit with misconduct, take a deep breath. This counsel applies to any disturbing event before or during trial. I have so often faced this temptation to strike back, or change course abruptly. When I have yielded to this temptation, I have almost always regretted it.

I know some lawyers who specialize in being outrageous. They will not be constrained by anything short of a contempt citation or professional discipline and perhaps not even then. They are often so practiced at their art that you could not "fight" them even if you wanted to throw out your case plan and do so. Against such an adversary, keep calm, keep on track, and keep on your plan.

Second, you can enlist the court's assistance, but there are limits on what that can accomplish. Your abusive adversary probably knows this. Case management and discovery conferences early in the litigation can help set limits on lawyer behavior. Strict and enforced rules about the timing and limits for discovery play an important role. Rules about deposition behavior help. The most effective judicial assistance must be sought and obtained before misconduct occurs and by participating in reform activities that set firm limits. The case management plans that came into being in the wake of the Civil Justice Reform Act of 1990 are worth studying. The best of those plans called for an early conference, discovery limits and—best of all—prompt judicial resolution of discovery disputes. For example, if a judicial officer is available to make telephone rulings during depositions, the telephone does not often ring because parties behave themselves.

Judicial intervention is problematic because the judge usually doesn't have time to sort out who is right and who is wrong. He or she wants the case to move forward, and is likely to behave like the parent who intervenes in children's fights by punishing both participants. Often, the judge's response is, "cut it out." Judges don't like to read pleadings full of mutual recriminations between the lawyers. So an effort to get help may in fact make you look worse.

Then there are those judges who do not seem to mind being misled. A short time ago, I argued a post-trial challenge to a criminal conviction. The prosecutor had failed to produce material exculpatory evidence in response to a defense discovery request. He had successfully moved to quash a defense trial subpoena by claiming that the material sought either did not exist or was not material. At trial, he had successfully cut off cross-examination by arguing that the defense had no factual basis for its questions. Well after the trial, a government document showed up in another case that showed the prosecutor had not been candid with the court. As pro bono counsel, I filed a petition for writ of error coram nobis. At oral argument, I thought that the trial judge would be offended by the prosecutor's conduct. He was not. It seemed that, like many judges, he had grown accustomed to revelations of lawyer misconduct of this kind, and wanted if at all possible to leave the verdict and judgment intact.

This sort of impatience with process values is not universal. Many judges have responded eloquently and forcefully to lawyer failures of candor. In the federal courts, the familiar three bases of sanctions are Federal Rule of Civil Procedure 11, 28 U.S.C. §1927 (which permits sanctions for vexatious conduct that complicates the litigation), and the court's inherent power. Under Federal Rule of Civil Procedure 60(b), lack of candor that amounts to fraud on the court can be redressed even years after the initial judgment. However, most judges, and not only those insensitive to process issues, insist that in seeking sanctions the movant be candid and thorough.

If the opponent's behavior includes ethical violations, you can invoke the aid of the bar, or file a motion to disqualify. I once represented five men charged with committing violent acts during a demonstration. The state attorney general held a number of inflammatory press conferences making false statements about the case. We filed a motion to disqualify him. He stepped aside rather than face a hearing on the issue.

When you sit down with colleagues to discuss the opponent's pattern of abuse, you must think through the entire range of potential responses and make your response part of your overall trial plan. Notice I have suggested sitting with colleagues. In the tournament of litigation, it is easy to generate a sense of outrage. The views of others can help you gain perspective.

Third, consider approaches outside the context of your particular lawsuit. The case-by-case effort to contain abusive behavior has a limited impact. I have suggested above that you look at procedural reforms. We should remember, however, that as a profession, we have organizational structures within which to express ideas about lawyer behavior. I know that debates about civility in litigation help to raise awareness of candor issues, and may help focus disapproval on unfair tactics. Such debates also help to draw important distinctions between abusive behavior—which is wrong—and vigorous, zealous advocacy—which is not only right but required by the rules of professional responsibility.

Fourth, where does your abusive adversary practice? Who are his or her friends, colleagues, superiors? Find out and talk to them. Point out the ways in which the behavior is actually taxing your adversary's client as well as yours, and impeding resolution of the case. Even in a large city, lawyer reputation is significant, and when bad behavior becomes the subject of general conversation, this may have a deterrent effect.

At trial, you will have opportunities to deal with lack of candor. Be careful not to use the "liar" epithet without the strongest possible justification. Speak instead in terms of promises kept and not kept. The opening statement was a promise. Did your adversary keep it? Did the witnesses, after direct examination and searching cross-examination, portray events in the way your adversary said they would. Has your adversary asked a question that assumes a fact not in evidence?

Has the summation contained inaccuracies? If so, you have the option to object during it, which is often not a good idea because the judge may simply say that the jurors' recollection controls. If the misstatement appears in a rebuttal summation, I would be more likely to risk objecting because one has no other way to make the point. In your own summation, you can use the techniques discussed elsewhere in this book—for example, in the next chapter's essays on empowerment and transparency—to emphasize that you and your adversary are advocates and that the jurors have ways to analyze the evidence and exhibits to see whose version of events is more near the truth.

The Judge's Candor

In trial, there are judges who not only try to prevent you from trying your case but actively seek to keep you from making a record on which you can appeal their errors. The judge may wave you to your seat without ruling on an objection. She may shut off lines of inquiry and refuse you the opportunity to make an offer of proof. She may make comments in the jury's presence that undermine your position. Your first job is to win your case to this jury rather than having to take an uncertain and expensive appeal.

You need courage, preparation, and a good sense of tactics. Politely insist on a ruling. Repeat your request. Pepper the judge with short written memos on contested issues. Present a written offer of proof. If the court has excluded the entire proposed testimony of a witness, such as an expert, hire a court reporter and do a Q & A with the witness back in your office, then put the transcript into the record. Confront the lack of candor in ways that build your record.

Sometimes a judge will attempt to signal counsel not to make a particularly strong argument, suggesting that to do so would be offensive and perhaps unnecessary. I appeared before a judge who, at the close of the prosecution's case, called counsel into the robing room and expressed grave doubts about the sufficiency of the government's proof. He said he had pretty well made up his mind to grant a judgment of acquittal on some counts of the indictment and did not see the point of taking up a lot of time arguing about it. He had, after all, heard the evidence. We reconvened in open court. I thought I should not waive any contentions or arguments, despite what the judge had said. He denied the motions for acquittal. I believe he always intended to do that, but can never be sure. Did I offend him by arguing?

I maintain my view that the judge was out of line in making his robing room comments with the intention of short-circuiting argument. One of my jobs as advocate is to protect the record made in open court by a court reporter, and not rely on winks, nods, and suggestions made in secret.

Judicial impatience or bullying is a form of lack of candor. I gave a talk at a judicial conference to lawyers who work on death penalty capital cases. I urged them to raise every conceivable point so that it could never be said that the client had waived a valuable right. After all, the procedural and substantive law of capital cases changes with every Supreme Court term, and a client cannot benefit from an issue not raised at the earliest possible procedural hour. As I left the room where I spoke, the chief judge of the circuit came up beside me and said, "Damn you, Tigar, you are telling these lawyers to fill up their briefs with meritless arguments instead of focusing on the main points." I replied blandly that the fault was not mine, but a system that enforces waiver rules in a macabre kind of "gotcha" game.

The judge and I were speaking of capital cases. But my view is that judicial impatience, when practiced as a device to control litigants and lawyers, should be excused as grumpiness. Judge Curtis Bok, in the preface to his book, *I, Too Nicodemus*, wrote these words, which a wise judge I know has in front of him on the bench as a stern reminder:

A good judge must have an enormous concern with life, animate and inanimate, and a sense of its tempestuous and untamed streaming. Without such fire in his belly, as Holmes also called it, he will turn into a stuffed shirt the instant a robe is put around him. The first signs of judicial taxidermy are impatience with trivial matters and the statement that his time is being wasted, for the secret of a judge's work is that ninety-nine percent of it is with trivial matters and that none of them will shake the cosmos very much. But they are apt to shake the litigants gravely. It is only his power over people that makes them treat him as a demi-god, for government touches them more perceptibly in the courtroom than at any other point in their lives. The cosmos is made up of little quivers, and it is important that they be set in reasonable unison. Show me an impatient judge and I will call him a public nuisance to his face. Let him be quick, if he must be, but not unconcerned, ever. Worse than judicial error is it to mishandle impatiently the small affairs of momentarily helpless people, and judges should be impeached for it.

We do read of and perhaps have experienced the worst forms of judicial lack of candor: the judge who takes bribes, who meets with favored lawyers ex parte, who favors those of a particular ideological or political persuasion. If you have the courage of which I spoke earlier, you will be willing to risk the consequences of reporting and opposing that behavior.

Your Client's Candor

Client anger can translate into client lying or client obstruction of justice. If the system seems stacked against you, or the process too long and expensive, moral relativism creeps in. The client may not level with you about the documents. The client may shade the truth. From the very first moment of your representation, you must explain the ethical, legal, and strategic pitfalls that await the litigant who is other than candid. You know these. Tell the client. People who lie or cheat get prosecuted. When liars and cheaters are exposed—and the adversary system makes the likelihood high—they lose their cases and get sanctioned by the court or subjected to civil liability for their misdeeds—including punitive damages. Punitive damages and sanctions for willful misconduct may not be covered by whatever insurance the client may have.

These elementary principles are both obvious and often ignored. High government officials and responsible corporate officers wind up escaping liability for serious misconduct but are found guilty of lying or covering up during the investigation that should have led to their complete vindication.

Remember, however, that contradiction is not lying. If a client says one thing to you at one time and another thing later, there may be a good reason for the change. It is important not to let the client get out there with a story until you have had the chance to make sure that potential contradictions of this kind don't see the light of day. I can remember a client who was convinced that he had attended a meeting at a certain time of day. Unfortunately, he testified to this version before I began representing him. Two witnesses contradicted him, saying that the meeting had in fact taken place at a different time, earlier that same day. The client had been led into error by reviewing his diary calendar. Originally the meeting was scheduled at the later time but had been moved. The problem could have been avoided by checking the client's version and conferring with him before he testified the first time.

Every trial lawyer knows that judge and juror perception of litigant candor is fragile thing. When one of "your" witnesses is seen to have been careless or economical with the truth, your entire team loses that perception of candor. Observing all the rules that have led up to this one is the only path to avoiding such a fate.

The Witness's Candor

How do we deal with the lying witness? We begin by making sure that the label fits. Not all mistaken people are liars. They may not have rightly observed, remembered, or related. Their error may be the result of a bias or prejudice that the witness carries but of which he or she is unaware.

In *Examining Witnesses*, I sounded a warning on this score:

> What do you want to accomplish with this witness? How will you argue that her testimony fits the story of

the case? How will the jury think about the story? You will seldom be able to argue that all the other side's witnesses are liars. Jurors are looking at witnesses and trying to figure out how to make sense out of what they say. They are trying to sort out contradictions and to explain them. By the time you rise to sum up, the jurors will have pretty well figured out what they think of each witness who has testified. The summation is a means of gathering facts for the jurors who lean your way, to use as ammunition in the jury room. It is a time to emphasize pieces of evidence that might be overlooked, such as documents that may have been alluded to but not published in full. It is a time to evoke the memory of testimony and to weave it into a coherent pattern.

Looking through the record you have made, you want to maximize the number of things that fit and minimize the number that do not. Claiming that all the opposing witnesses are liars violates this principle and calls on the jurors to perform the distasteful job of labeling an entire group of testifiers as perjurers. You will, in trying cases, come to label many witnesses as liars and should not shrink from this duty when the occasion demands. The occasion demands, however, far less frequently than some people think.

In sum, in most instances the witness's error is not mendacity. She may not have been in a position to observe events properly, and your cross-examination will focus on the objective facts that show this. Or, she may not remember well, and you will have at hand a prior statement that more clearly describes what she observed. Her testimony may have been vague, and when clarified will shine light where you want it.

But if you face a liar, consider pointing that out forcefully and early in your examination. Terry MacCarthy and I agree on this point, and we have both approved of the cross-examination that begins, "Mr. X, you are a liar, aren't you?" or "Mr. X, can we agree that you are a liar?" If you have the means to impeach an answer other than "yes," go ahead. Once you have decided to go after the liar, you must show the jury that the label fits, not simply tell them that it does. Your witness file must have contradictory prior statements. It must contain objective evidence that contradicts or casts doubt. It must show the jury how the witness's tale has developed and changed in response to pressure or hope of benefit. Books on technique abound; one of mine is cited in the Notes.

Notes

- *Chambers v. NASCO, Inc.*, 501 U.S. 32 (1991) (court's power to impose sanctions on various bases, including inherent power).
- *Demjanjuk v. Petrovsky*, 10 F.3d 338 (6th Cir. 1994) (candor to adversary and court).
- For detailed consideration of the lying witness, see *Examining Witnesses*, Chapter Eight.

Empowerment

The Experience of Being a Juror

I recall a presentation about voir dire by a lawyer whose name I no longer remember. He imagined group inquiry of potential jurors.

> Good morning. You have all been called in here to decide this very important case. The judge will not tell you what the rules are until you have listened to all the evidence, so you really won't have any idea about what you are going to decide until the very end. That's OK. Just listen, remember everything and maybe it will all become clear in the end. I am going to ask you some questions. This is a case about science. Do any of you have any prejudices about the wave theory of light as opposed to the particle theory? I take it by your silence that none of you do. And how about people being incinerated when a reactor blows up? I see a few shocked expressions, but nobody raises their hand, so I guess that is all right also.

For many jurors, the trial process is alienating, in the precise sense that they feel separated from the formal structure within which they are supposed to be acting. They seek connections and often cannot find them. Your responsibility as advocate is to make the presentation of evidence, argument, and legal principles not only compelling and accessible. You must respect the jurors' judgment and help them to connect to what they are hearing and seeing.

You do not achieve this connection by condescension. Rather, at each point in the trial, you enlist the jurors' rational faculties, and you make sure your performance is memorable.

The jurors are witnesses to the events of trial. Eye- and ear- witnesses are regarded as the most valuable contributors to juror understanding. Our rules of evidence are based on that premise. Yet we also understand all the human fallibility of such evidence, based on memory, perception, meaning, and bias. We know how to reinforce witness impressions of events, to preserve those impressions for recounting at trial, supplemented by visual aids. We tend to forget that jurors share the same frailties as our witnesses, and need reinforcement also.

In the unfamiliar territory of trial, jurors will look for clues about what they should do. Yet jury studies also show that jurors regard their service as one of the most significant experience of their lives. They appreciate that they are exercising the power of judgment on behalf of the sovereign. They are bringing community sentiment into the decisional process. This was the image of jury trial shared by those who wrote the Constitution and the Bill of Rights, and one can hear echoes of it in post-trial juror interviews today.

Your job as trial counsel is to tap into that sense of civic responsibility and to reinforce it. The jurors have power. They may be reluctant to exercise it. They may have preconceptions about legal principles that stand in the way of applying the rules fairly. You must empower them to pronounce judgment in your client's favor.

I see this issue most clearly in criminal cases. Prosecutors are wont to focus on social danger. It takes courage for jurors to say, on behalf of the community, that there is a reasonable doubt, even though they may feel at some level that it is more probable than not that the defendant committed a crime. Even in civil cases, however, there are often hot button issues more or less close to the surface. In almost every automobile accident trial, there is a subliminal message about insurance rates and unworthy plaintiffs. Questions of race, gender, ethnicity, or religious affiliation may be present depending on the nature of the claims and defenses and who the witnesses are.

The first meaning of empowerment, therefore, is to reinforce the juror sentiment to represent the community honorably. A second meaning is to be prepared to make rational factual arguments in favor of a result—that is, to participate in the deliberative process. We want our trial work to create memorable episodes of testimony and exhibits that jurors will retain and be able to use as they decide the case with their colleagues. This second form of empowerment requires not only thorough preparation, but a mode of presentation that shows the jurors what matters and why it matters. I have called this latter consideration transparency.

Transparency and Empowerment

"Look, Ma, no hands!" cries the child on the bicycle. There are times in trial when we just want to turn to the jury and mouth "yes!" Or do one of those end-zone things that we see on TV. This sort of thing is not allowed. Each element of advocacy has a function, and one element cannot, should not, be made to do the job of another. Cross-examination cannot do the work of summation. You cannot stop the cross from time to time and tell the jurors what point you think you have just made.

Some years ago, in a libel trial, a federal judge permitted the lawyers to interrupt their presentations at will and talk to the jury about where they thought the case then stood or what purpose had been served by what the lawyers or witnesses had just done or said. This experiment has been repeated in some complex cases, by permitting mini-arguments at various points in the trial, but has not been widely copied. The order in which witnesses are presented, imaginative use of exhibits in both direct and cross-examination, and a solid opening statement that puts matters in perspective can accomplish the task of keeping the jurors focused on the narrative that an advocate is trying to tell. Also, I worry that mini-arguments actually interrupt the flow of trial, and interfere with the coherence of presenting a story.

Voir dire provides an introduction to the case, or at least to the issues that may affect juror behavior. Opening statement announces the structure within which the case will be tried. In direct examination, you will use prologue, loops, and transitions to guide juror attention, as discussed in the chapter on Structure. You may introduce cross-examination themes one at a time. In cross-examination, you may even be able to let the witness explain to the jury why his or her own testimony should be discounted.

In the Terry Nichols case, a main government witness was Michael Fortier. Fortier was a long-time friend of Nichols' alleged coconspirator Timothy McVeigh. By the time of Nichols' trial, McVeigh had already been convicted. After the Oklahoma City bombing, Fortier held out against FBI efforts to get him to tell his relationship to McVeigh, while conducting a series of telephone conversations with family and friends bragging about how much he knew and how he would become rich and famous as a witness in the case.

Fortier's methamphetamine-driven dreams came to an end when he and his wife received subpoenas to appear before the Oklahoma City federal grand jury that was hearing evidence about the bombing. In an Oklahoma City motel, Michael and Lori Fortier resolved to tell what they knew in exchange for leniency. They called the FBI office. Two agents came to see them. Fortier said in effect, give me and Lori immunity and we'll give you McVeigh. The agent said that the FBI could not give immunity and that they already had McVeigh sewed up. Fortier heard the message and he and Lori spun a story about Terry Nichols.

My cross-examination of Fortier had several themes, which are addressed at greater length in *Examining Witnesses* and *Trial Stories*. But one important idea in that cross was empowerment, and transparency was the means to achieve it.

I wanted to empower the jury to argue rationally about the believability of what Fortier said at trial. I had two themes.

The first theme was to show how Fortier's story about Terry Nichols had shifted bit by bit as he continued his discussions with the FBI and traveled from significant location to significant location with a team of agents. I could show this progression by using Fortier's prior statements and the FBI 302 reports of interview generated based on agent conversations with him along the way. I wanted the jury to follow the changes in Fortier's story a step at a time. I hoped that they would at some point see not only the contradictions in his story but the entire line of attack. I wanted jurors to say to themselves that they could see how the FBI agents and Fortier worked together to alter what he was willing to say.

The second theme was based on Fortier's recounting of what Timothy McVeigh had allegedly said about Terry Nichols' involvement in the bomb plot. I wanted the jury to have tools with which to separate out the issues of his and McVeigh's credibility. So I asked him if he understood that the jury has two questions here about what to believe about what McVeigh allegedly said. The first is whether the jurors can believe Fortier when he tells us about McVeigh. And the second is whether, if McVeigh said something, McVeigh was telling the truth or not. Remember that under the rules of evidence you can attack the credibility of a hearsay declarant by many means, including this one. I think it is difficult for jurors to see the inherent weaknesses in co-conspirator declaration testimony. The admissibility rules are difficult for judges and lawyers to parse. So the examination must help the jurors acquire a sense of skepticism, and provide them with tools to analyze the believability of what they are hearing. Tools of analysis empower; unadorned invitations to disbelieve do not.

Having got Fortier to agree that his and McVeigh's credibility were both issues for the jury, I could ask, "Timothy McVeigh was a liar, wasn't he?" Then, I could list the instances in which McVeigh had lied to Fortier, had induced Fortier to commit illegal acts, and had otherwise comported himself in a way that would lead a person to disbelieve what he said.

In another case, I had an IRS special agent on the stand, who relied for his summary testimony on what an accountant had told him. I noted the ways in which the accountant was, by his own admission during the agent's own investigation, untrustworthy. I then asked, "Agent, would you buy a used car from Mr. X?" The agent fumbled and finally blurted out, "If the price was right." The jurors said after trial that they thought that question was the best one asked at trial and served to shine the light on the agent's testimony.

A Template for Empowerment: Expert Witness

At the end of this section is an excerpt from the beginning of an adverse examination. The witness is an FBI agent who was in charge of developing systems for intercepting and recording telephone calls. The examiner has obtained documents that show that the system was flawed in several important ways. After this initial encounter, he will confront the witness with these documents, which are in evidence because they come from the FBI's files.

This examination suggests a structure for expert witness adverse or cross-examination. To do this sort of questioning, the litigation team must assemble all the relevant information about how the witness and his or her colleagues performed the tests, collected the data, or otherwise did their job. Next, the team must make a list of "optimal" standards for doing the job that were not observed.

This examination also shows you what characteristics you want your own experts to have: teachers by inclination, not condescending, happy to defend their views with good humor and good examples.

The examination begins by getting the witness to agree that each item on the list of "optimal" standards is correct. Where the witness will not agree, the examiner will either (a) seek agreement on a slightly different but nonetheless acceptable definition, or (b) nail down the disagreement so that the examiner's own witness can take up the battle.

Next, the examiner takes the witness through the steps of his or her work, showing ways in which the principles of "optimal" work were not observed. This examination is "adverse" because the impeaching documents were not produced in discovery until long after the initial direct and cross and the trial judge would not permit recall for further cross-examination. But the principles are the same.

The case was *U.S. v. Lynne Stewart*, in which there were some 88,000 telephone intercepts on several recording systems. One must recall in this context that a digital recording is a "writing" within the meaning of the "original writings" or "best evidence" rule. The judge had refused to require the witness to be recalled after the government turned over evidence indicating that his prior examination had been less than complete. So the defense called him as an adverse witness. The examination is long and technical. If you are not interested in telephone tapping and voltage drops, and most people are not, try to imagine this sort of inquiry being made of a laboratory technician, a physician, or some other expert with whose work you are more familiar. The object here is to have a list of optimal or "good" practices, and to use it as the basis for asking questions to which the witness is almost compelled to give the answers you want.

MR. TIGAR: Lynne Stewart calls FBI Agent Michael Elliott.

DIRECT EXAMINATION BY MR. TIGAR:

* * *

Q: And, sir, you had spent some time preparing for your reappearance here today?

A: Yes.

Q: Did you have an opportunity to discuss the subjects upon which you might be examined with members of the prosecution team before coming here this morning?

A: Yes, I did.

Q: About how long did you spend doing that?

A: I was in New York a few weeks ago and I was probably with them for a couple of hours. And maybe some conversations on the phone, not a lot of time.

Q: Did you have some opportunity to spend time with them within the last couple of days?

A: Only this morning prior to coming to court.

Q: And you declined an opportunity to meet with the defense, is that correct? [We had offered him that opportunity.]

A: Yes.

Q: Since you were last here the government has provided you with documents relating to problems with the systems used to record calls for this case, have they not?

A: Yes.

Q: And you have reviewed other documents in the course of assisting the government in complying with various document requests, is that correct?

A: Yes.

Q: Before I show you some of those documents, sir, I'd like to ask you about the goals of an electronic surveillance system, the subject about which you testified the last time you were here. Sir, an optimal system for recording telephone calls would accurately and completely record all the calls on the target telephone, correct?

A: No. It would only record the calls that were presented to the collection system.

Q: So it would accurately and completely record the calls that were over—that were designed to be overheard on the target telephone, correct?

[Note that he would not accept the characterization in the first question. That is all right, so long as the examiner works with him to get him to accept some characterization that fits the examiner's objectives.]

A: Yes. Yes.

Q: It would accurately determine whether a call it was recording was incoming or outgoing, correct?

A: That was the intent.

Q: Pardon?

A: That was the intent of the system.

Q: Yes. It would accurately determine the telephone number of the calling party, correct?

A: Yes.

Q: To the extent permitted by the phone systems the calling party was calling, it would accurately determine the telephone number of the called party?

A: Are you referencing caller ID?

Q: Yes.

A: Yes.

Q: And you recall telling us last time that some foreign telephone systems did not permit the FBI's equipment to record the telephone number of the called party, do you remember that?

A: Yes, I remember.

Q: An optimal system would not break the recorded calls into multiple parts, would it?

A: No, that's not necessarily true.

Q: Is it your goal to record a call without gaps in the recording?

A: Yes, that is true.

Q: So an optimal system would not have gaps in any calls that it recorded, correct?

A: No, that's not true either.

Q: All right. Under what circumstances would an optimal system permit there to be gaps in the parts of the calls that were being recorded?

[The examiner does not care what the answer is. The evidence will show there were gaps. The gaps are either a fault in the system as designed, or are gaps that may be unavoidable in that system but may nonetheless be significant.]

A: The—whether the recorder is on or off is determined by the device that's in the field that I previously testified about called the loop extender. That loop extender emits a tone. That tone determines whether a recorder comes on or the recorder goes off. It's not the collection system. It's the tone that's there. The presence of the tone coming from that loop extender that's on the telephone pole tells the recorder to go off. The absence of the tone causes the recorder—the recording system to come on. It's that tone that causes breaks in conversations or breaks in recordings.

Q: Now, when you say "the loop extender," you're talking, sir, about a circumstance where someone depresses the—what we call a switch hook on the telephone, correct?

A: No, sir.

Q: What are you talking about?

A: In my previous testimony I—there was a graphic that was displayed. And we showed where a technical agent of the FBI would go to the telephone pole or the pedestal box nearest the telephone that's to be intercepted and they would apply a device called a loop extender. That's the device that isolates the target telephone line and allows the FBI to listen in on those telephone calls. And it's that device that emits this tone that turns the recorders on and turns the recorders off.

[He is taking the long way around, but wait and see how it comes out.]

Q: And isn't—but isn't it a fact, sir, that what—well, let me ask you this: The target telephone is the telephone you're trying to record, correct?

A: That would be the—the target telephone would be the telephone that is mentioned in the court order that the intercept is against.

Q: And when the person on that telephone takes the phone off hook, something happens, correct?

A: Yes, sir.

Q: What happens is that the voltage drops, correct?

A: That's correct.

Q: And the voltage drop is the thing that triggers the recording device back at FBI headquarters, correct?

A: No, sir. The voltage drop is what signals the tone to go away. It's the tone that's on the line back to the FBI field office. It's the absence of that tone that causes the recorder to go on and go off.

[Again, he is making it harder, but all he did was add a step to the analysis.]

Q: So we put in another step. When the target telephone is off the hook, there's a voltage drop, correct?

A: Yes, sir.

Q: The voltage drop in turns causes something to happen with the bridging device, correct?

A: That's correct.

Q: And that's the tone, correct?

A: Yes, sir.

Q: Now, in the course of a telephone call, if a person calling depresses their switch hook to activate call waiting or three-way calling, that also causes a voltage drop, correct?

A: What the switch hook does is it simulates an onhook/offhook instance. If one holds it long enough, if you hold the switch hook long enough and you're not quick with it, the voltage can return. So it's not a voltage drop. It's like you're going back on hook so the voltage would return if they hold the switch hook too long. If they don't, if they do the switch hook very quick, then thus you get that conference call or that three-way call.

Q: Now, when you were last here, sir, you told us about that and you said that a system could stop recording after a disruption very temporarily for a second or two or three, correct?

A: Yes.

Q: An optimal system would not permit gaps in recording of let us say a minute, right?

A: I don't know that.

[He doesn't know it because his technical expertise is a little thin, but the next question clears it up.]

Q: As an investigator, an experienced investigator, you wouldn't want a system that causes gaps in recordings of a minute, would you?

A: Well, my preference would be to have a system that would record an entire telephone call. That would be the best evidence.

Q: So that was my question, sir. As an investigator, you wouldn't want there to be gaps, correct, of a minute?

A: I would not want there to be gaps.

Q: Now, your optimal system, returning to that, would accurately archive all the recorded calls so that they could be retrieved later, correct?

A: That would be the intent of the system.

Q: And you want to be able to retrieve the calls later because the prosecutors that were going to present a case would want them, correct?

A: Yes, sir.

Q: And you would want to retrieve them all later because if a case is brought, defendants, whose liberty is involved and they're in a trial, you want to make production to them, correct?

A: Yes, sir.

Q: And you would want to be able to retrieve all of the archived materials, right?

A: Yes.

Q: And in that archiving you want to have the calls archived on reliable storage media, correct?

A: Yes.

Q: And when you take that storage media, be it a tape or an MO disk out, you want to have it accurately reproduce the archived calls so that the recordings can be played and understood, correct?

A: Yes.

Q: You want a system that minimizes software failures, correct?

A: Yes.

Q: You want a system that minimizes hardware failures, correct?

A: Yes.

Q: You want a system that if there are software or hardware failures has redundancy so that no calls are lost, correct?

A: Redundancy is determined by the office, but, yes, you would like to be able to ensure that no telephone calls are lost.

Q: And in a secured system, you want the system to have security, correct?

A: Please repeat that.

Q: You want your system to be secure from outside tampering, correct?

A: Yes, sir.

Q: And you want to be able to know that any outside tampering that took place would be detectable, even if it was done by cleared personnel, correct?

A: Yes, sir.

Q: And your optimal system would also have an external database, would it not, so that a—one could tell if a call or recording period was missing?

A: Not necessarily.

Q: You don't regard that as necessary, external database?

A: I—the system is what it is. And I'm not—I don't understand your question.

Q: Would you as a person in charge of meeting the FBI's needs want there to be a database of calls that were recorded that is external to the system; that is, external to the archived media and keeps a record of what was recorded?

A: No. That was the purpose of the archived media, so that we would not have to have a huge external database forever. The archived media was intended for that.

Q: And so the archived media—external to the archived media, you didn't have a database, correct?

A: It was not designed with a database, that's correct.

[He does not concede the need for an external database, but any defense IT expert will say that any information storage system must have some external system that provides a backup record.]

Don't Send Flowers, Plant Seeds

Throughout the trial, in opening statement, witness examination, and closing argument, you are the jurors' surrogate. You raise the issues that are decisive. You isolate what is important and contested from that which is trivial and conceded. In a play we wrote, Kevin McCarthy and I put these words in the mouth of the nineteenth century Irish lawyer Daniel O'Connell, based on a speech O'Connell had made:

> You all know how to argue to a group of people who are set against your most basic beliefs. You never get them by showing them that you have got the matter all worked out, in a set speech like the catechism—or whatever might be the Protestant equivalent of the catechism.
>
> We can't drag the jurors along with us. Make them imagine that their movements are directed by themselves. Pay their capacities the compliment of not making things too clear. Rather than elaborate reasonings, throw off mere fragments, or seeds of thought. These will take root and shoot up into precisely the conclusions we want.
>
> Sometimes you will do this soft and soothing. But there will be times, when you suspect the jury's purity, to remind them of their juror's oath. Then approach and defy them to balance for an instant between their malignant prejudices and the clear and resistless justice of the case.

We can study rhetorical styles of political, spiritual and other teachers. We can ask ourselves whether those styles are appropriate in jury argument. In 2004, Senator Barack Obama gave the keynote speech at the Democratic National Convention. The style and substance of that speech were inspiring. In his 2008 presidential primary campaign, Senator Obama's speeches struck deep chords, even among seasoned political observers. A professor of rhetoric applied the term "consilience" to Obama's technique. Consilience is a term coined in the nineteenth century and refers to a process of bringing together diverse strands of learning and insight into a new paradigm or intellectual structure.

In an article on slate.com, Jack Shafer wrote:

> No less an intellect than *The New Yorker*'s George Packer confesses that moments after a 25-minute campaign speech by Obama in New Hampshire concluded, he couldn't remember exactly what the candidate said. Yet "the speech dissolved into pure feeling, which stayed with me for days," he writes.

George Packer's response to Senator Obama is not the sort of response you want from jurors, or at least not entirely. Of course, your summation must empower jurors by setting emotional anchors: the sense that trust has been breached or not, of their own power to decide the facts, of confidence in their sense of justice and injustice, of confidence in their ability to separate believable from less believable. To do this, you will call upon shared ideas and ideals from diverse sources. But "pure feeling" will not sustain your cause as the jurors begin to deliberate. There are cases with lightning-fast verdicts. Most of the time, the jurors will be arguing inference from witness testimony, the meaning of exhibits, the tenor of the judge's instructions, and all the other elements that will persuade them one way or another. Your rhetoric must empower them for that task, even as its emotive power impels them to perform it in the proper spirit.

You must know two kinds of words: hedgehog words and fox words. "The fox knows many things, but the hedgehog knows one big thing." Isaiah Berlin took this aphorism from Archilochus, an ancient Greek poet, to describe two ways of looking at history. I seize upon them to illustrate two ways of looking at the evidence in your case, from the beginning of your work and into closing argument.

You must have a hedgehog idea, in hedgehog words. That central idea is the reason why your client is entitled to the justice you seek. It is an idea that resonates with jurors, and motivates them to get down to work in deliberations to put facts and law together and reach a verdict. But, as I have said often, and in different ways, you must show the jurors the tools they need to do their work—the key items of evidence and important principles of law in the jury instructions. You want fox words, fox ideas, bringing together analysis and experience to see the way through.

Daniel O'Connell is right, and so is Barack Obama, each in his own way. O'Connell talks of how to empower by providing tools of reasoning and analysis. Obama invokes major concepts about justice, suggesting that these are major organizing principles. The "fox ideas" help jurors grasp the elements of narrative to be found in exhibits and in witness testimony. The "hedgehog idea" comes along and gives a reason to view these elements in the way that supports the advocate's position.

Notes

- See Jack Shafer, "How Obama Does That Thing He Does," http://www.slate.com/id/2184480

Presentation

This chapter is brief. If you have heeded the previous eight principles, you are ready to present voir dire, opening, direct, cross, and closing. All that remains is to remind you of how to keep those principles alive and at work during the trial.

Place of Presentation

Presentation *has* a place. It takes place during settlement negotiations, in mediation that seeks settlement, in court-annexed arbitration, in mock trial rehearsals for the main event, and at trial. Presentation is the last of the nine principles, which is fitting because presentation will fail unless the advocate observes the other nine principles, and because most cases will be settled short of actual trial.

Presentation also occurs *in* a "place," a setting. Typically, that setting is a "courtroom." But that word, "courtroom," denotes many very different kinds of places. There are the intimate, rounded shapes of Frank Lloyd Wright's courtrooms in Marin County, Calif. There are the cavernous ceremonial rooms on the first floor of Foley Square, New York. There are high-tech courtrooms with every kind of gadgetry, and courtrooms without any such ornament— where you must bring your own pad and easel if you want to create or show a visual aid. There are courtrooms where counsel for one side or both sides are far from the jurors. The witness chair may be set in any of dozens of possible relationships to the jurors. Every time I appear in a courtroom, I am impressed by how its shape, arrangement, style, and acoustics affect the way the lawyers do their jobs, and how the deciders perceive the process. If I am to appear in a courtroom where I have never been, I get there early to get a sense of what the space represents and signifies.

Presentation also has a place defined by the judge's rules concerning how lawyers move. In some jurisdictions, lawyers examine witnesses from a seated position at counsel table. In other places, counsel must stand behind or near a lectern. Some judges permit counsel to rove around. In some courts, one may not approach a witness even to show an exhibit. One gives the court clerk or bailiff the exhibit, and he or she shuttles it back and forth.

If you are permitted to move around, do so economically, as discussed in the chapter on Structure. Every one of your movements, gestures, and expressions must have a purpose; ask others to observe you to make sure you have learned this principle. When you rise to object, do so in an easy motion. Move comfortably and easily in the courtroom. Take your time. Look like somebody who is in charge of events, confident but not overbearing. These admonitions sound trivial—until you see an advocate who is not heeding them.

Before approaching the witness, wait until you have something that you want the jury to know the witness must see and that will be significant. Example:

Q: Didn't you write a memo on April 21, 1995, about Ms. Smith's job performance?

A: I don't remember.

Q: May I approach?

Court: Yes.

[Walk up to the witness and stand next to him without blocking the jury's view of the witness.]

Q: I show you what has been marked at Plaintiff's exhibit QQ. Look at it, please, and just tell us whether that refreshes your recollection that wrote a memo on April 21, 1995.

A: Yes. Okay.

[Now go back to the lectern. The jury wants to see this "tennis match" and it is better if you are not hanging over the witness's shoulder, even if the court would let you do that.]

You and your team must be comfortable in whatever physical setting is provided and under whatever rules are enforced there. You want everyone on your team within your field of vision. You want to be able to see the other side, the jury, and the court. That means lead counsel sits in the chair that is the corner seat, or the closest equivalent, given the courtroom arrangement. When you sit there, you are visible, but you also can keep everything in the courtroom under observation.

Whenever a member of your team is performing, all eyes should be on him or her. Scribbling notes or messing with exhibits distracts from what must be the most important courtroom event at that moment. The jurors will naturally move their gaze to the distracting activity and away from the main event.

The lead lawyer must be in charge and must be listening at all times. That means you don't want anybody talking in your ear. So the whispered conversations are all initiated by the lead lawyer. That is, if you want to talk to the client—or anybody else on the team, you can do so. If they want to communicate with you, they make a note. Those notes are put in the agreed place if you are on your feet doing something. While you are seated at counsel table, your client can pass the notes to you directly—understanding that the number of notes must be kept to a minimum.

In this physical space, you sit with the client. A basic principle of trial is that you start by being credible. You transfer that credibility to your client. For me, this means that in the courtroom, you relate to your client as the most important person in the lawsuit. Your team stands up to greet the client, unless you all walk in together. You all say good morning.

Remember, the jury will not hear from the client until the case is well along, and in a criminal case perhaps not at all.

They form their impression of the client through observing you and your team, and your direct and cross-examination.

I have no problem with putting a hand on the client's shoulder during tough moments of the trial. Of course, the client should know not to react too visibly during the testimony with gestures of approval or dismay. A normal and understandable reflection of emotion is fine.

The place of presentation may or may not be equipped for the modern technology of Power Point, the ELMO device, TV monitors, or even an overhead projector. I have the advantage, in thinking about the range of presentation options, of having come to lawyering when the overhead projector, the blackboard, the easel and expensive charts were all one had available. This perspective does not, I hope, make me unreasonably suspicious of modern techniques, but it certainly makes me doubt the wisdom of overloading your presentation with gimmicks.

Dead Reckoning

I wrote in *Examining Witnesses*:

> Sailors use a method called "dead reckoning." You know where the voyage began. You know your course and speed, and you have some idea about the current and the side-setting effect of the wind on your sails. You can plot an approximate, dead-reckoning fix. But you cannot be sure where you are until you sight land or a fixed object on the sea, such as a navigational buoy.

In trials, we have only an approximate "dead reckoning" sense of where we are and how well we are doing with the judge and jury. I know some lawyers and clients have "shadow juries." The media covering a high-profile trial hire lawyers to comment on the proceedings. But none of this so-called expertise has any guarantee of accuracy.

You call on your experience as a trial lawyer, and that of your team, to estimate each day how well your case plan is doing. Now, take the analogy to sailing a bit further. Suppose there were buoys marking your passage from one port to another. You could measure progress by noting the numbers and configuration of the buoys, on the outgoing and return trips.

In your trial plan, you must establish buoys to mark positions. You do this with exhibits and trial events that have visible significance, and that are easily recalled in summation to give the jurors a point-by-point way of reconstructing trial events in the image you would want them to have.

Remember, the jurors are witnesses—with eyes and ears—to the trial events. As lawyers who present testimony and exhibits, we understand the fallibility of human memory for things heard or seen, and we know how memory of specific events can be reinforced. We litigate the admissibility of eyewitness identification, and cross-examine witnesses for signs of influence exerted upon them. We seek jury instructions warning jurors of the fickleness of memory and the way that it can be shaped by external events.

We present trial evidence by making as clear as possible all the ways in which the jurors are to evaluate what they are seeing and hearing. This is transparency. Second, we equip jurors to deliberate intelligently and productively about what they have seen and heard. This is empowerment. In voir dire, we empower jurors by inquiring about how they make decisions. In opening statement, we acknowledge that the evidence is in dispute and are candid about possible flaws in our case. Almost every witness's version can be challenged in some way. The meaning of almost every document can be debated. And this jury is here to resolve the contradictions and make a decision.

On direct or cross-examination, mark as many events as possible with exhibits. If the events took place in an office, have a diagram of that office. Mark the relevant places and admit the exhibit. If there was an admissible memorandum, admit it. These exhibits are marker buoys that you will retrace in summation.

Organize your examination and announce the organization. Tell the jurors what to expect:

> First, I am going to ask you about who you are and how you came to be in that office. Then I will put some questions about your co-worker Mary Smith. Finally, we will talk about the atmosphere in that office.

Think of your case visually. Think of its constituent parts so you can identify them as you go along. The goal here is to be able to stand up in summation and say:

> Members of the jury, I am an advocate. That is, I am here to support our side. When you go to the jury room, you

will be grading my paper and the other side's paper. You may ask, "How do I know if I can rely on what Mr. Tigar said?" I hope you will ask that, about me and any other lawyer who addresses you. In that hope, I am going to go through many of the exhibits that are in evidence in this case. You will be able to look at these exhibits in the jury room and see whether I am getting it right. Often during the trial, I would put an exhibit up while a witness was testifying, to support or emphasize some point, or maybe give a point of reference. You might look back and remember more clearly what a witness told you by remembering that there was an exhibit that went along with the testimony.

Exhibits: Presentation by Showing and Telling

This is what I said about exhibits and demonstrative evidence at the Nichols trial. You can read my entire summation in a book published by the Professional Education Group, or online. There is more about demonstrative evidence in my books *Examining Witnesses* and *Persuasion: The Litigator's Art*. It is a little hard to follow this excerpt because you have to imagine what the exhibits to which I referred looked like, and the names are not familiar. But you can see the way in which I invited the jurors to focus on the specific content of exhibits that the government had been content to summarize with charts. I was inviting the jurors to parse these documents themselves, as they evidently did in several long days of deliberation before acquitting Mr. Nichols of most of the charges against him. This part of the summation, after a four-month trial in which the jurors heard more than 200 witnesses, is not dramatic. To be sure, we used dramatic reference, emotional anchors. But we also respected the idea that the jurors would want to work through the evidence and be very sure of their conclusions before they came to a verdict. The "we" is literal, as co-counsel Ron Woods and I each did parts of the summation:

> During this summation, we're not going to use any demonstrative evidence; that is to say, we're not going to use any charts or diagrams or summaries. Why not? Because I tell you frankly that those charts or diagrams or summaries can mislead you, because they represent selections by lawyers, not in bad faith, but as advocates, trying to advocate a position, as to what you ought to pay attention to. We're going to try to show you some of those exhibits that you'll have the opportunity to look at.

Then, as I went through the summation, I used only those exhibits that jurors would have a chance to look at in the jury room in their deliberations. Where the prosecution had used a summary or item of demonstrative evidence for illustrative purposes, I contrasted their excerpted version with the actual original taken as a whole.

Presenting Witness Examination

I sum up the principles of witness examination in ten ideas about presentation, assuming that you have respected all the other rules before the moment of presentation arrives. One could write an entire chapter about each one of these ideas, and, indeed, I have written about them in greater detail in other books. But here they are, simply as mnemonic devices or as the equivalent of a wallet card that reminds you of key ideas:

The Revised Standard Ten Commandments Of Cross-Examination—and Direct As Well

1. Perception
2. Memory
3. Meaning
4. Veracity, to include implied bias
5. Factual basis for opinions and conclusions
6. Qualifications
7. Procedures
8. Transparency
9. Jury Empowerment
10. But the greatest of these is: The Theory of Minimal Contradiction (also known as, don't try to eat soup with a fork)

The first four principles remind us that witnesses can be mistaken for reasons other than bias or deliberate falsehood. Explore all the bases of potential contradiction. The next three principles apply most cogently to expert witnesses. However, all witnesses may express conclusions and opinions within limits. All witnesses are qualified or not qualified to tell us what they say—physically, mentally, by virtue of their ability to observe and recall what they are recounting. Expert witnesses use procedures to arrive at results. Lay witnesses are subjected to procedures for recording and recalling facts and preparing them to testify. Transparency is the subject of much of Chapter Nine. Jury empowerment is the theme of this chapter and the one before it.

I have discussed the theory of minimal contradiction in the chapter on Structure. Also, I wrote in *Examining Witnesses*:

> What do you want to accomplish with this witness? How will you argue that her testimony fits the story of the case? How will the jury think about the story? You will seldom be able to argue that all the other side's witnesses are liars. Jurors are looking at witnesses and trying to figure out how to make sense out of what they say. They are trying to sort out contradictions and to explain them. By the time you rise to sum up, the jurors will have pretty well figured out what they think of each witness who has testified. The summation is a means of gathering facts for the jurors who lean your way, to use as ammunition in the jury room. It is a time to emphasize pieces of evidence that might be overlooked, such as documents that may have been alluded to but not published in full. It is a time to evoke the memory of testimony and to weave it into a coherent pattern.

Looking through the record you have made, you want to maximize the number of things that fit and minimize the number that do not. Claiming that all the opposing witnesses are liars violates this principle and calls on the jurors to perform the distasteful job of labeling an entire group of testifiers as perjurers. You will, in trying cases, come to label many witnesses as liars and should not shrink from this duty when the occasion demands. The occasion demands, however, far less frequently than some people think. ...

I call my view the "theory of minimal contradiction."

You do not need to carry the jurors to a completely different world view than the one advance by your opponent. The tournament of trial is limited by rules that confine the dispute in various ways. You are looking for that perceptual shift that dictates a different result.

Markers, Tone, and Words

The excerpt above is from an exhibit-driven summation, which combined different techniques of persuasion. In a case with many documents, such a summation inflicts death by a thousand (paper) cuts. The summation plan was to build issue upon issue, giving the jurors the material they could review during deliberations to verify what the advocate was saying. The exhibits you use are, to refer again to the dead-reckoning metaphor, the marker buoys you laid down during the direct and cross-examination of witnesses.

I am not the only advocate to note that the days of efful-
gent tub-thumping summations are almost over. There is a
canon of dramatic presentation: If you rise to an emotional
pitch too early, you cannot sustain the emotion. You have no
place to go. A courtroom is a small space, compared to a tent
revival. Have you noticed how candidate speeches recorded
at outdoor events and played on radio or television cause you
to recoil a bit? Too loud, too boisterous, though perfectly
adapted to the place where given.

Empowering means reasoning. The more difficult and
inherently emotion-laden the issue, the more that you must
be sure to call upon the quiet force of facts to carry the jurors
along. Give them the peace of your mind.

Choice of words is vital. You read court opinions and
begin to use lawyer words, such as utilized, purchased, exit-
ed, structured, instead of used, bought, left, shaped. Cast
these out of your vocabulary. When you argue to a jury or
judge, you will not write out your speech. Therefore, you
must have a large store of good words to use without having
to read from a prepared text.

Here is a telling example I how important the right word
can be. William Butler Yeats' poem, "The Second Coming,"
ends with the famous lines

And what rough beast, its hour come round at last,
Slouches towards Bethlehem to be born?

The original draft, in Yeats' handwriting, is in Dublin. He
first wrote "marches," and changed the word to "slouches."
Changing this one word—which Yeats then used in the

poem's subtitle—greatly enhanced the drama of his poem. "Slouches" gives us a very different mental picture of this "beast" than "marches."

Presenting Yourself

The jurors will hear what you say, and see what you show them. But they will also judge who they think you are. Juror comments are surprisingly insightful, and often blunt:

- "a real classy lady"
- "she's the one I would want defending me!"
- "did he think we are stupid?"
- "too much use of innuendo"

Whether you are conscious of it or not, the jurors are asking themselves whether you can be trusted. They may read significance you're your demeanor and gestures.

Over the years, I have worked with and studied different images about presentation of self. I am taken with George Winthrop's 1630 work, "City Upon a Hill." He presents the image of a community that is healthy within itself, but also stands as an example to those who pass by. Another image is Jacques Derrida's positing someone coming forward to say, "Je voudrais apprendre à vivre enfin," which translates to "Finally, I want to learn how to live." But "apprendre" can also mean "teach," so Derrida captures the idea that in the process of living our lives we both learn and teach at the same time. As lawyers, we do our work in a public forum. I wrote this in *Fighting Injustice*:

As advocates, we are condemned to signify. That is, we are communicators. We are trying to convince this or that decider to rule for our clients. That is a limited though vital meaning of signifying. We also signify in a broader sense. The kind of work we do, the cases we take, the way in which we accept or defy injustice: the entire body of our work speaks to the world about our values. It tells the world whether and how much we believe we can get justice in the present state of things. Our advocacy to deciders is better if we continue to see the links between theory and practice, and continue to understand the narrow and broad senses in which we signify.

The quality of your advocacy, and your leadership and mentoring of other advocates, are forms of presentation of self. They give you satisfaction beyond that of winning a client's claim for justice, or earning a respectable fee. I sometimes say that a trial lawyer is a large blob of ego suspended over a chasm of insecurity. That metaphor describes the adrenaline-fueled engagement in litigation combat. It is easy for a trial lawyer to think that his or her responsibility ends with doing the best for this client, this day, in this forum. That is a false conclusion. Long-term success in this profession depends on understanding justice in human relationships, and that understanding must begin with personal and professional dealings. Success depends on having forums where justice is spoken of and done, and that depends on fighting to keep such forums open and available.

These are some of the reasons why this book is titled
Nine Principles of Litigation—and Life.

Notes

• In my book, *Persuasion: The Litigator's Art,* see the heading
  "The Speaker and the Hearer."

Index

1-2-3 approach, 205, 210

ABA Guidelines (for capital defense), 90, 153

ABA Journal, 9

Adams, John, 68

Adversary system, 15, 16, 32, 34, 53, 56, 137, 193, 220, 240

Altgeld, John P., 47-49

Altman, Robert, 145

Apartheid, 17, 27, 61-62

Arnold, Richard Sheppard, 135

Art of Cross-Examination, The, 215

Attorney for the Damned, 46

Axam, Tony, 97, 145

Ball, Joe, 60

Beck, Philip, 207-208

Beckett, Samuel, 25, 26

Berger v. United States, 83

Berlin, Isiah, 265

Best, Judah, 31

bin Laden, Osama, 9, 11, 12-13, 16

Bok, Judge Curtis, 238

Brennan, William J., 30

Bright, Myron, 135

Brougham, Lord, 78

California Supreme Court, 60

Cather, Willa, 13

Charleston Five, 83-84

Chavez, Cesar, 99

Chavez, Fernando, 99

Chesterton, G.K., 16, 138, 153

Cicero, 21

"City Upon a Hill," 280

Connally, John, 99, 126, 230-231

Cooper, Grant, 57-61

COYOTE, 18-19

Curran, John Philpott, 45-46

Daily Oklahoman, 107-119

Darrow, Clarence, 29, 46-49, 65, 99

Debs, Eugene V., 47-48

Delgado, Richard and Jean Stefancic, 186-187

Demjanjuk v. Petrovsky, 83

Diamond, Bernard, 123

Doyle, Sir Arthur Conan, 151

Dryden, John, 25, 26

Emerson, Thomas, 39

Erskine, Thomas, 43-45, 55, 61

Euripides, 22-23

Examining Witnesses, 214, 215, 219, 241, 249, 271, 274, 277

FBI (Federal Bureau of Investigation), 125-127, 147, 199, 216, 249-251, 252, 253-262

Federal Rules of Civil Procedure

    Fed. R. Civ. P. 11, 234

    Fed. R. Civ. P. 16(b), 173

    Fed. R. Civ. P. 26(f), 173

    Fed. R. Civ. P. 60(b), 234

Federal Rules of Evidence, 193

    Fed. R. Evid. 612, 219

Fighting Injustice, 280-281

Finch, Atticus, 29

Fortier, Lori, 249

Fortier, Michael, 125-126, 249-251

Frazier, Ken, 54

Fry, Christopher, 157

Fry, Stephen, 228

Fuentes v. Shevin, 14-15

Furman v. Georgia, 75, 76

Gentile, Dominic, 81-82, 84, 178

Gentile v. State Bar of Nevada, 84, 178

Glaspell, Susan, 6

Goldstone, Richard, 32

Grotius, Hugo, 36, 38, 39

Haddon, Hal, 85

Hamilton, Andrew, 40-42, 45

Hand, Learned, 34

Higginbotham, Patrick, 135

Hirschhorn, Robert, 112

Hoffman, Julius, 62

"horizontal" view of justice, 36-39

Hossack, Margaret, 5-9, 16, 47

Iowa Supreme Court, 5

I, Too, Nicodemus, 238-239

Jackson, Michael, 209

Jacobsen, Jake, 126

Jamail, Joe, 208

Jefferson, Thomas, 43, 69-71

Johnson, William, 69-71, 72

Kittredge, William, 182

Kunstler, William, 62

"Lady's Not for Burning, The," 157

Lanier, Mark, 206-207

Lawrence v. Texas, 147

Lee, Wen Ho, 34

Lee, Wilbert, 72

Liar, The, 228-229

Lindsay, Vachel, 48

MacCarthy, Terry, 200, 215, 243

Mandela, Nelson, 61

Matsch, Richard, 81, 103-104, 110, 118

McCarthy, Kevin, 64-65, 263

McElhaney, James, 214

McVeigh, Timothy, 104, 109, 126, 150-151, 210, 249-251

Miami Herald, 72

Miller, Gene, 72

Milton, John, 123

Monet, Claude, 141-142

Morris, Gouverneur, 43

"Murders in the Rue Morgue, The," 187

National Law Journal, 51

New York Times, The, 52

New Yorker, The, 264

Nevada Supreme Court, 82

Nichols, Terry, 52, 73, 77, 80, 85, 95, 103, 108-119, 125-126, 127, 147, 149, 150, 210, 249-250, 274, 275

Nuremburg, 32

Nussbaum, Martha, 35, 38

Obama, Barack, 264-265

O'Connell, Daniel, 65, 263, 265

"Of the Law of War and Peace," 36

Packer, George, 264

Persuasion: The Litigator's Art, 143, 166-171, 274

Petronius, 21

Pincham, Eugene, 148

Pitje, Godfrey, 61-62

Pitts, Freddie, 72

Poe, Edgar Allen, 187

"Pro Murena," 21

Raise the Bar, 13

Reynolds v. United States, 33

Robertson, Cathy, 149

Rodney, Caesar, 70-71

"Salt of the Earth," 100

Scalia, Antonin, 30, 37

"Second Coming, The," 279-280

Selvin, Herman, 60

Shafer, Jack, 264

Shipley, D.W., 44

South Africa, 27, 61

Susman, Morton, 105

Susman, Steve, 208

Sweet, Ossian, 46

Tambo, Oliver, 61

Tigar, Jane, 95

Thinking about Terrorism, 69

Trial Stories, 249

United States v. Coplon, 34

United States v. Lynne Stewart, 252-262

U.S. Supreme Court, 14, 30, 33, 37, 69, 75, 82, 83, 90, 130, 147, 175, 178, 185, 238

"vertical" view of justice, 36-39

Vioxx, 53-54, 206-208

Wellman, Francis, 215

Williams, Edward Bennett, 30, 95, 126, 128, 135, 199-200, 213, 230-232

Wilson, Bill, 213

Wilson, Harold, 128

Winthrop, George, 280

Wood, John H., 134-135

Woods, Ron, 53, 80, 110, 134, 212, 275

Yeats, William Butler, 279

Yevtushenko, Yevgeny, 26

Zenger, John Peter, 40-43

About the Author

Michael E. Tigar is Professor of the Practice of Law at Duke University School of Law, and Professor Emeritus of Law at Washington College of Law, American University, Washington, D.C. He has held full-time positions at UCLA and The University of Texas. He has been a lecturer at dozens of law schools and bar associations in the United States, Europe, Africa, and Latin America, including service as Professeur Invité at the Faculty of Law of Université Paul-Cezanne, Aix-en-Provence. He is a 1966 graduate of Boalt Hall, University of California, Berkeley, where he was first in his class, Editor-in-Chief of the law review and Order of the Coif.

He has authored or co-authored twelve books, three plays, and scores of articles and essays. He has argued seven cases in the U.S. Supreme Court, about 100 federal appeals, and has tried cases in all parts of the country in state and federal courts. His latest books are *Trial Stories* (2008) (edited with Angela Jordan Davis), and *Thinking About Terrorism: The Threat to Civil Liberties in Times of National Emergency* (2007).

His clients have included Angela Davis, H. Rap Brown, John Connally, Kay Bailey Hutchison, the *Washington Post*, Mobil Oil, Fantasy Films, Terry Nichols, Allen Ginsberg, Leonard Peltier, the Charleston Five, Fernando Chavez and Lynne Stewart. He has been chair of the 60,000-member Section of Litigation of the American Bar Association, and chair of the board of directors of the Texas Resource Center for Capital Litigation.

In his teaching, he has worked with law students in clinical programs where students are counsel or law clerks in significant human rights litigation. He has made several trips to South Africa, working with organizations of African lawyers engaged in the struggle to end apartheid, and, after the release of Nelson Mandela from prison, to lecture on human rights issues and to advise the African National Congress on issues in drafting a new constitution. He has been actively involved in efforts to bring to justice members of the Chilean junta, including former President Pinochet. Of Mr. Tigar's career, Justice William J. Brennan has written that his "tireless striving for justice stretches his arms towards perfection."

In 1999, the California Attorneys for Criminal Justice held a ballot for "Lawyer of the Century." Mr. Tigar was third in the balloting, behind Clarence Darrow and Thurgood Marshall. In 2003, the Texas Civil Rights Project named its new building in Austin, Texas, (purchased with a gift from attorney Wayne Reaud) the "Michael Tigar Human Rights Center."